Yin and Yang of Life

Yin and Yang of Life
UNDERSTANDING THE UNIVERSAL NATURE OF CHANGE

by Joseph K. Kim, OMD, Ph.D.
and David S. Lee, MD, OMD

Copyright © 2008 by Joseph K. Kim and David S. Lee

All rights reserved. This book may not be reproduced, in whole or in part, in any form or by any means electronic or mechanical, including photocopying, recording, or by any information storage and retrieval system now known or hereafter invented, without written permission from the publisher, Heal and Soul, LLC.

YIN AND YANG OF LIFE

Published by
Heal and Soul, LLC.
16545 Ventura Blvd., Suite 24
Encino, CA 91436

www.healandsoul.com
www.yinyangoflife.com

Typeset by D. Dog Design
Cover design by D. Dog Design
Printed in the U.S.A. by Delta Printing Solutions

Library of Congress Control Number: 2010910112

ISBN 978-1-4507-2574-3

Disclaimer: The advice given in this book regarding diet, tea, and exercises does not replace proper medical care. Nothing contained herein is intended to diagnose, treat, prevent, or cure any disease. Before following the recommendations in this book, please consult your healthcare practitioner if you have any medical condition. The author and the publisher are not liable for any loss, damage or injury in any manner whatsoever resulting directly or indirectly from the use and application of the book.

*Dedicated to the followers of Tao
whose love and compassion help maintain peace,
balance and harmony in the world*

Contents

Introduction 1
Chapter 1: Basic Principles of Yin and Yang 9
Chapter 2: Yin and Yang of Human Beings 19
Chapter 3: Yin and Yang of Sex 33
Chapter 4: Yin and Yang of the Brain 46
Chapter 5: Yin and Yang of Food and Diet 52
Chapter 6: Yin and Yang of Politics 85
Chapter 7: Yin and Yang of the Economy 90
Chapter 8: Yin and Yang of Perspective 94
Chapter 9: Yin and Yang of Music 99
Chapter 10: Yin and Yang of Wave 106
Chapter 11: Yin and Yang of the Universe 109
Chapter 12: Yin and Yang of Sleep 119
Chapter 13: Yin and Yang of Performance Enhancing Drugs 131
Chapter 14: Yin and Yang of Obesity 147
Conclusion 165
Notes 167
Select Bibliography 169
Acknowledgments 171
About the Authors 173

Authors' Note

Words in this text that have no direct equivalents in English, such as Tao, Tai Chi, Qi, and Jing have been capitalized. The physiological actions of organs as interpreted in eastern medicine are different from that of western physiology. Thus, organs such as "Kidneys" and "Heart" have been capitalized to differentiate them from western anatomical organs.

The advice given in this book regarding diet, tea and exercise does not replace proper medical care. Nothing contained herein is intended to diagnose, treat, prevent, or cure any disease. Before following the recommendations in this book, please consult a physician if you have a medical condition.

Parts of this book have been previously published in Korea under the title *Science and Tao of I Ching*.

An Introduction to Yin and Yang

> The principle of yin and yang is the natural order of the universe, the basis of all things, mother of all changes, and the source of life and death.
> *Chapter 5, Yellow Emperor's Inner Classic*

Most of us at some point in our lives have asked philosophical questions about life itself. Our underlying motivation is a quest for self-knowledge, self-identity, self-awareness and self-realization. We wonder "What is the essence of existence? How can we understand ourselves and the universe more fully? What lies at the heart of chaos, conflict and the world's woes?" We also search for answers that will help us lead healthier, fuller and more prosperous lives.

In the East, the answers to our many questions can be found in the concepts defining a universal principle of change called yin-yang theory. This theory of universal duality is so deeply ingrained in eastern culture that it is safe to say that it is the foundation of every aspect of eastern civilization: from art, music, architecture and dance to sex, politics, economics, astronomy and diet.

The influence of yin-yang theory is not limited to the population of East, however. It has influenced the thinking of many great western minds, illuminating paths to discovery. Basic tenets of yin-yang theory lie at the heart of German mathematician and philosopher Gottfried Wilhelm Leibniz's binary system and Albert Einstein's theory of relativity. It also influenced the work of Friedrich Hegel, Karl Marx and Carl Jung, who were all life-long students of yin-yang theory.

What are Yin and Yang?

Mathematically speaking yin and yang are the binary language of the universe defining all phenomena in opposing paired sets. Examples of these dualities are (in yang - yin order) day and night, male and female, hot and cold, hard and soft, good and evil, true and false. We see these opposing pairs in mathematics and science: addition and subtraction, acid and alkaline, energy and matter, positive and negative, protons and electrons. We can also find these pairings in philosophical and religious pairings such as heaven and hell, thesis and antithesis, spiritualism and materialism, life and death.

In the most simplistic terms, yin and yang are the energetic axes of the universe. They are the polar, yet complementary forces that are the basis of every aspect of existence. Yin and yang are not only static pairings, however; they exist in relation to and because of one another. One cannot exist without the other. They are two sides of the same coin and the two opposing aspects of all matter and phenomena. It is impossible for yin to exist without yang and vice versa. Nothing in the universe escapes this principle of simultaneous duality.

In addition to being relative opposites that define one another, yin and yang are also dynamic, shifting, generating and evolving energies. In other words, there exists an intimate yet active bond between them. On one hand, yin and yang oppose one another, creating conflict, tension, friction and discord. On the other hand, they complement one another, creating dynamic harmony, balance, equilibrium and stability. This paradox is the very nature of yin and yang, either positive or negative depending on the perspective of an observer. Both positive and negative actions result from this dynamic and harmonious alliance. The bonding and interaction of yin and yang are absolutely essential for existence and the sustenance of all life and universal activity.

The dynamic interplay of yin and yang results in the diversities of nature's shapes, colors, forms and characteristics. It is these differences that give life its meaning and purpose. Without such variances life would be dull and boring, or worse—it would not exist at all.

A Brief History of Yin and Yang

Some believe the origin of the concept of yin and yang began with ancient shamans and occultists thousands of years ago, although no one knows for sure. The beginnings of this remarkable concept are shrouded in myth and legend. However the first application of the principles of yin and yang can be observed in the *I Ching*, also called the *Book of Changes*. Popularly known as a book of divination, the *I Ching* is traditionally believed to have been created approximately 5,000 years ago and actually contains the highest teachings of all of the eastern classics. It is also generally considered the oldest book in existence.

As its name suggests, the essential theme of the *I Ching* is change, the change brought about by two forces: yin and yang. The word or ancient Chinese pictogram for "yang" originally described the sunny side of a hill while "yin" represented the shady side. The meaning is that yang describes light and sunshine and yin describes darkness and shadow. It is from these simple descriptions that yin and yang came to represent all phenomena and matter, the entirety of the cosmos.

Tao and Tai Chi

Tao and Tai Chi are two profoundly important ideas in the study of eastern philosophy, religion and culture. These terms define the universal nature of all things material and energetic. For many, these concepts are difficult to understand because the nature of what they attempt to define is elusive. Nevertheless, they are the most essential concepts in eastern philosophy and must be understood before all else.

According to the *I Ching*, Tao is synonymous with a concept of totality, a concept which serves as the foundation of eastern philosophy and culture. Tao speaks of oneness and the interconnectedness of all things. Literally translated as the "path" or "way," Tao is the path that all things must travel to fulfill their true nature. Tao defines the way things are.

The nature of Tao is elusive and difficult to understand. It is said that all paths lead to Tao and that Tao is the totality of all possible paths. Eastern philosophical traditions also teach that ultimately there is only one path and it is called Tao. Tao is considered to be the only path because it is thought to be the original source of everything that exists. These apparent contradictions are indicative of the difficulties that arise from attempts to explain the true meaning of Tao with language.

Tao is the beginning and the end, one thing and all things. It is the cause and effect; existence and non-existence; the tangible and the intangible; the concrete and the abstract; what is known and what is unknown; the past, present and future; space, time and what lies beyond.

Tao is the principle that guides all things and yet there is nothing fixed about it. Since the only constant in the universe is change, the only absolute of Tao is that it is always changing.

Tai Chi is translated to mean the "Supreme Ultimate." Simply stated, Tai Chi is a symbolic or pictorial representation of Tao. Because Tao is so elusive and intangible, the Tai Chi symbol was created to express a more concrete embodiment of the Tao. Tao and Tai Chi are used interchangeably. The subtle difference is that Tai Chi is used by the *I Ching* and Tao by those training to become enlightened. Since the *I Ching* is a book that expresses Tao in symbols or codes, all principles of the *I Ching* are contained within the Tai Chi symbol. Like Tao, Tai Chi defines the universal nature of all things material and energetic. Tai Chi is the unity, oneness and totality of the universe. It is the alpha and omega, the beginning and the end. It is the undifferentiated totality.

Yin and yang are the way in which Tao and Tai Chi play out in nature. Thus, the *I Ching* describes their relationship by stating "the alternation of yin and yang is called Tao." It also states that "Tai Chi produces yin and yang; when Tai Chi moves, it becomes yang; when it is still, it becomes yin." All changes in nature occur due to the interaction between these two forces.

The power of yin-yang theory lies in its ability to describe changes via the various ways that yin and yang relate to one another. Yin-yang theory describes six such relationships, called the Six Basic Principles: (1) mutual opposition; (2) mutual dependence; (3) mutual consumption and support; (4) mutual transformation; (5) infinite divisibility; and (6) inversion (form-function relationship). We will discuss these principles in detail in chapter one.

The Yin-Yang Symbol

The yin-yang symbol is one of the oldest and best known representations of the universal nature of change. It is also known as the Tai Chi symbol. It represents the dynamic interplay of polar, yet complementary forces in nature, both creating and destroying one another. The white swirl represents yang and the black, yin. The red swirl is yang and the blue is yin. The yin-yang symbol reveals the perfect balance of opposites and demonstrates the quintessential notions of balance, equality, equilibrium and harmony. The line dividing the two halves is s-shaped to represent unending dynamic change. It also represents the flow of time, depicting the changes that occur with time.

Figure 1   **Figure 2**

Figure 1 is the more common depiction of the yin-yang symbol with the white swirl ascending in a clockwise (yang) direction. Because the swirl is in a vertical position (yang - movement) heading up towards heaven (yang) it is considered more yang in nature and more representative of a dynamic state of change than is Figure 2, which has horizontal (yin - stability) swirls and is considered more yin in nature. The red (fire/yang) top swirl and blue (water/yin) bottom swirl of Figure 2 represent a more static, peaceful universal state. In addition the swirl in Figure 2 is moving in a counterclockwise (yin) direction. Despite their differences, both symbols depict the very essence of the *I Ching*, the principles of yin and yang. The swirling motion illustrated in both figures portrays the transformation of yin into yang and yang into yin, as energy transforms into matter and matter into energy.

The white dot in the black swirl and the black dot in the white swirl illustrate one of the Six Basic Principles: yin within yang and yang within yin. The dot portrays the opposing aspect that is within every situation, circumstance, process or phenomenon. It is the representation of the statement "Nothing is ever all good or all bad;" or "Everything contains the seed of its opposite."

Why study Yin and Yang?

The study of yin and yang is a path to self-discovery and self-understanding. It can help you gain a deeper understanding of yourself, others, and all of creation.

It will help you to see the interconnectedness of everything, and to understand your relationship to yourself, others and the rest of world. It can help you open up to seeing the bigger picture and to truly appreciate the beauty and elegance of existence. It will ultimately lead to an understanding of what you may call Tao, God, or the universe. As many sages and masters throughout history have declared, "Every one of us contains a world within." We are a microcosm, a miniature universe, or a model of the universe. The knowledge of yin and yang will help us realize this profound truth.

As they describe the principles of universal change, yin and yang will help us understand the ceaseless motion and transformation that takes place in this world and will help us remember how fleeting life can be. The only constant in life is change. Nothing escapes this principle.

Studying and practicing the principle of yin and yang in our lives means we are following the laws and living in tune with the flow of nature. It is in fact the most simple, natural and practical way of living. Yin and yang create and sustain the universe and all its inhabitants. This knowledge is the key that will unlock the door to your true nature and the nature of the universe.

Explore and discover the yin and yang in your environment, at home, in people, and in nature. See how it creates, balances and harmonizes in order to express beauty and elegance in everything. But notice also how an imbalance in yin and yang can create chaos, conflict and turbulence in life. See and feel the yin and yang aspects of your life and learn to appreciate this duality. Ultimately, you will discover the dynamic interplay of yin and yang within you and learn to become one with the Tao.

Yin and yang are not merely theoretical concepts to brood over. In order to be understood they must be practiced and applied to all aspects of life. Just as it is necessary to do many math homework assignments before you really understand mathematical concepts, yin-yang theory must be constantly applied to diverse subjects to truly gain an understanding of its brilliant concepts. To this end, this book covers a wide variety of subjects and shows various ways that yin-yang theory can be applied in order to better understand life. Subjects range from the macrocosmic to the microcosmic, including the universe, economics, politics, health, diet, sex and many other aspects of daily life.

We have written this book to help readers understand yin and yang not

AN INTRODUCTION TO YIN AND YANG

only from a philosophical and theoretical perspective but also from a very practical perspective. It is our sincere hope that readers will gain a deeper understanding of yin-yang theory and be able to apply its concepts to their own experiences. Once you arrive at a thorough understanding of the yin and yang binary language, you will find that the decisions necessary to live a balanced life will be illuminated before you. You will also find your goals within easy reach.

Yin and Yang of Life

CHAPTER 1
The Basic Principles of Yin and Yang

Yin and yang are the Universal Binary Language. Like the binary code that is the fundamental language of all computer systems, yin and yang are the language with which we can interpret and understand all of the complexities of our lives and the world around us.

Computers store vast amounts of information in very small spaces. They also perform extremely sophisticated calculations. Although the power of computers is enormous, their basic language is composed of two characters: 0 and 1. Regardless of size or complexity, all input and data translated by computer systems is inevitably broken down into established series of these two characters. This allows ease of understanding for anyone familiar with the binary code. It is also the most efficient and coherent method of storing information.

In much the same fashion, life, nature and the universe can be understood more easily when you are versed in the Universal Binary Language of yin and yang. Regardless of the complexity of the situation, once all of life's attributes are translated into the language of yin and yang, you will be able to gain deeper insight into your path and move easily in the direction of your goals.

In short, yin and yang are the code, ruler, gauge and matrix with which you can convert, measure, calculate, unravel and interpret all information. From common to extraordinary, cheap to precious, simple to complex, vulgar to noble, divine to diabolical, concrete to mysterious, everything is a manifestation of yin and yang.

To understand yin and yang, it is first necessary to comprehend the fundamental characteristic pairs and their polarities. The following table shows some of the general characteristics, functions and directions of yin and yang (Table 1.1):

	Yin	Yang
General Characteristics	static	mobile
	darkness	light
	cold	hot
	thick	thin
	turbid	clear
	dense	sparse
	invisible	visible
	rigid	flexible
	Yin	**Yang**
Function	passive	active
	suppression	excitation
	regression	progression
	preserve	transform
	completion	initiation
	discontinuous	continuous
	sustaining	changing
	yielding	proceeding
	resting	acting
	nourishing	protecting
	responding	commanding
	decaying	flourishing
	restraint	action

THE BASIC PRINCIPLES OF YIN AND YANG

	Yin	**Yang**
Direction	downward	upward
	internal	external
	centripetal	centrifugal
	front	back
	inside	outside
	north	south
	west	east

Table 1.1 Yin-Yang Characteristics

The following table illustrates other yin-yang pairings relating to various universal phenomena (Table 1.2):

	Yin	**Yang**
Universal Component	substance	energy
Quantum Mechanics	particle	wave
Cosmos	Black Hole	White Hole (Big Bang)
Human Beings	body	mind
	female	male
Mind	subconscious	conscious
Spirit	corporeal soul	ethereal soul
Organisms	plants	animals
Car	braking system	propelling system
Stock Market	bear	bull
Computer	memory	calculating function

Table 1.2 Yin-Yang and the Universe

The Six Basic Principles

Yin and yang are more than fixed, static pairings as they represent not only matter and form but also energy and function. In fact, it is the interaction between these two forces which brings about all the changes that occur in nature.

The Six Basic Principles of yin and yang describe the six ways that yin and yang interact. It is the formulation and representation of these relationships that give power and meaning to yin-yang theory. These principles are: (1) mutual opposition; (2) mutual dependence; (3) mutual consumption and support; (4) mutual transformation; (5) infinite divisibility; and (6) inversion (form-function relationship).

(1) Mutual Opposition

The most basic yin-yang principle, Mutual Opposition, states that everything in the universe has an opposing counterpart. Everything, no matter how complex or basic, pure or adulterated, magnificent or minute, has a relative opposite. Thus, all phenomena in the universe can be seen as either yin or yang. For example, phenomena are either positive or negative, male or female, up or down, open or closed, outside or inside, day or night, acid or alkaline, loved or hated, joyful or sad, etcetera.

(2) Mutual Dependence

The principle of Mutual Dependence states that yin and yang depend upon one another. So in addition to having an opposing counterpart, all things also depend upon their opposing counterparts. This means that nothing can exist without its opposite and everything is defined by its opposite. For example, there can be no front without a back, top without a bottom, inside without an outside. In other yin-yang pairings the dependence is indirect, but no less inescapable. For example, animals (yang) depend on plants (yin) for oxygen and plants depend on animals for carbon dioxide; male and female organisms depend on one another for the continuation of their species.

(3) Mutual Consumption and Support

The principle of Dependence explains that yin and yang depend upon one another. It does not, however, describe how yin and yang depend upon and affect each other. The principle of Mutual Consumption and Support elaborates on this relationship by defining the interaction between yin and yang as consumptive yet nurturing.

Yin and yang have a reciprocal relationship. The strength of yin or yang depends on the weakness of its counterpart. When yin grows stronger, yang is consumed and becomes weaker and vice versa. Viewed from another perspective, however, the yin and yang relationship can be seen as supportive. When yin is consumed, yang becomes stronger to fill the void. The same is true of yin when yang is consumed. An oil lamp provides an accurate illustration of this reciprocal relationship. In the lamp, the oil is considered the yin aspect because its nature is substantial. The flame is considered to be yang because fire is characterized by movement, heat and light. The flame needs to consume oil to burn. But if the burning flame consumes all of the oil the flame will also vanish because the oil supports the flame. In addition, if the flame is extinguished both the oil and the lamp will lose their functional purpose.

(4) Mutual Transformation

Not only do yin and yang define, consume and support one another, they also transform into each other, defining their relationship as one of conservation and exchange. When yin reaches its extreme it transforms into yang. When yang is at its zenith it transforms into yin. The transformation of yin into yang and yang into yin allows the energetic cycle to continue moving forward.

One example of this principle is seen in Einstein's famous theory of relativity ($E=mc^2$), which states that matter (yin) and energy (yang) are different forms of the same thing and can transform into one another. Another example is seen in the discovery by quantum physicists that electrons act as both particles (yin) and waves (yang). In 1926 Werner Heisenberg formulated his Uncertainty Principle, which stated that the position and momentum of these electrons can not simultaneously be known. The reason behind this phenomenon is in the constant transformation of yang into yin and vice versa. In the infinitely microscopic world of quantum physics transformation is taking place at such a rapid speed that it is impossible to ascertain both the momentum and position of a particle at the same time. This is, in fact, one principle of change mentioned in the *I Ching*.

In daily life this principle of change is more gradual. The speed with which this process takes place is dependent upon the number of factors that are being altered. While one electron transforming from a particle into a wave may take an immeasurably short amount of time, day turning into night (yang to yin) and its reciprocal takes 24 hours. The waxing and waning of the moon and the changes of the seasons are other examples of this gradual yin-yang transformation.

The principle of Transformation is actually one of conservation. By transforming into each other, yin and yang are recycled and conserved. If yin and yang only consumed each other, they would eventually become depleted. The mutual transformation of yin and yang prevents this from occurring. By constantly changing from one to another, often in a cyclical or pendulum-like pattern, a dynamic balance is maintained.

(5) Infinite Divisibility

The principle of Infinite Divisibility states that nothing in the universe is either purely yin or purely yang. Regardless of how yin or yang a phenomenon appears to be it can always be further broken down into smaller yin and yang components. For example, although daytime is yang, it can be divided into two periods: sunrise to noon and noon to dusk. Sunrise to noon, because it is the brightest time of the day, is considered to be yang within yang. Noon to dusk, the period in which darkness overcomes daylight, is considered to be yin within yang. The nighttime may similarly be divided. Within these divisions are further divisions. Any given hour, minute or second can be broken down and viewed in relation to its position on the spectrum of darkness and light and assigned more yin or yang properties. Anything can be broken down in this manner until we arrive at the smallest known particle, which is constantly transforming between yin and yang.

(6) Inversion

The Inversion Principle is the most elaborate and profound principle of yin-yang theory. Inherent to this principle is the importance of the observer when assigning yin or yang to things. Like the four blind men who each reached very different conclusions about the nature of the elephant they touched depending upon what part of the animal they felt, people interpret situations in various ways depending upon their experiences and perspectives. In the same way, objects and situations have inherently opposing yin and yang characteristics depending upon the aspect of the object or situation being explored and the perspective of the observer. This is what the Inversion Principle describes and it does so in three ways by exploring: (A) Form and Function; (B) Alternative Positions; and (C) Essence and Manifestation.

THE BASIC PRINCIPLES OF YIN AND YANG

(A) Form and Function

One fundamental tenet of the Inversion Principle is that the form or structure (yin) of something is inversely related to its function or energy (yang). Depending on the relative perspective of the observer, the same phenomena can appear yin if its structure is being analyzed and yang if its function is analyzed, or vice versa. Following are examples of this contradictory nature of form and function in many different aspects of ordinary life.

1. Size and Speed

The bigger (more yang) something is, the slower (more yin) its speed tend to be, and the smaller (more yin) something is, the faster (more yang) its speed tend to be.

Let's take a simple example of a bus versus a sports car. In terms of size, the bigger an object the more yang it is. So, a bus is more yang than a sports car. In terms of speed, however, the faster an object, the more yang it is. So a sports car is more yang than a bus.

Most of the objects we see around us have a stable form; when they move, their velocity is easily measured because they are relatively big (yang with regards to form), and thus slow (yin with regards to function). In the world of quantum physics, electrons and other particles are so small (yin with regards to form) and they move so fast (yang with regards to function) that their position (yin) and momentum (yang) cannot be measured simultaneously.

2. Strength and Density

Density is yin. Strength is yang. The denser an object, the more yin it is. Conversely, the stronger an object, the more yang it is. When analyzing wood and metal from the perspective of density, metal is more yin than wood. However, analyzing these two materials from the perspective of their relative strength, metal is more yang because it is stronger.

3. Visibility

In general, things apparent to the eye are yang and things that are not visible are yin. In this respect, the body is yang in relation to the mind. However, from the perspectives of speed, weight and denseness, the mind is much more yang than the body.

The relationship between Form and Function and the perspective of the observer are important to remember when assigning yin or yang to any object or situation in order to truly understand the workings of the universe.

(B) Alternative Position

In addition to Form and Function, the Inversion Principle also reveals the relationship of yin and yang by comparing various positions, such as the upper and lower, front and back, and internal and external.

A famous maxim, attributed to Hermes Trismegistus, states "As above, so below; as below, so above," meaning that the same patterns exist on every plane of reality. For example, the human body reflects the patterns of nature which in turn reflect universal patterns. Atoms reflect patterns of human cells which in turn reflect patterns of the human body. Each new level of existence is a reflection of and carries the same information as the next or previous level. Modern fractal theory describes this as "self-similarity." Eastern philosophy acknowledges that the microcosm reflects the macrocosm and vice versa, forming a foundation for practices such as reflexology and iridology.

Applying the Inversion Principle to this axiom, however, we see how perspective changes outlook. Let's look at the qualities of softness and hardness and how they manifest in nature.

Watermelons have hard external shells, but inside they are soft. The same is true of cantaloupe, honeydew and coconut. Peaches, on the other hand, are soft on the outside, but inside they have a hard pit as do apricots, plums and nectarines. Fish are soft on the outside but have hard vertebrae inside. Shell fish such as oysters, clams, crabs and lobster, however, are hard externally but soft inside. We see this in the human body as well. The skull is hard on the outside, but the brain inside is soft. The abdomen is soft, but inside is the hard lumbar spine. These examples show how an object that appears yang externally will be internally yin and vice versa.

The Inversion Principle is also found when comparing the upper and lower region of the same thing. Many trees have green leaves (yang) that absorb light from the Sun (yang). Underneath, however, are their dark roots (yin) that absorb water and minerals from the Earth (yin). Turtles have a hard top shell (yang) but a very soft underbelly (yin). Seasons in the Northern and Southern

THE BASIC PRINCIPLES OF YIN AND YANG

Hemispheres are also inversely related. Summer in the north is winter in the south and vice versa. In addition, storms in the Northern Hemisphere rotate in a counterclockwise direction while those in the Southern Hemisphere rotate clockwise.

The Inversion Principle also manifests when comparing the front and back sides of our bodies. According to yin-yang theory the front of the body is yin because it is "soft" and more vulnerable than the back (yang) which contains the spine and powerful back muscles. The upper body is considered yang compared to the lower body (yin) because it is higher and its movements are freer.

Because the nature of yang is expansive and yin is contractive, things that protrude are considered yang and things that sink inward are yin. When looking at the human body, the chest and buttocks protrude, highlighting the Inversion Principle. In the front of the body (yin region), the chest (upper, yang region) sticks out but in the back of the body (yang region), an inversion takes place and the buttocks (lower, yin region) stick out. This is the way nature balances yin and yang.

(C) Essence and Manifestation

Perhaps the most complicated aspect of the Inversion Principle, Essence versus Manifestation, conveys the idea that what is apparent to the naked eye (yin/form/structure) is actually the opposite of the intrinsic nature (yang/function/energy) of any given thing. This principle is the foundational concept giving rise to statements such as "putting on a façade," "wearing a mask," and "don't judge a book by its cover," which convey a profound universal truth.

Water, for example, appears soft and malleable and conforms to any container into which it is placed. It is, however, the catalyst for any hardening process. Consider cement or clay. Both will remain in the form of powder until they are mixed with water. Life, too, requires the presence of water. Scientists search the universe for water as an indication of the potential of other life forms. The reason water is necessary is that although it initially seems to soften things, it actually causes things to gather and harden (yin). Only through such yin actions can a birth take place. Water provides the contractive (yin) force necessary for a birth (yang) or an explosion (yang) to eventually take place. This is the intrinsic nature of water; soft on the outside and hard on the inside.

Metal is just the opposite. While it appears hard, any metal put into a fire will melt into liquid. So, while metal appears to be a hard substance, its true nature is soft.

People are much the same. While a person may seem hard on the outside, in general those people are covering up a very soft internal personality. Conversely, people who may appear soft by nature may carry a great deal of strength inside.

The Inversion Principle emphasizes the perspective of the observer when assigning yin and yang qualities to any given object or situation. It reminds us that different perspectives produce different conclusions. When added to the other five principles, it completes the theory of yin and yang giving us the guidelines necessary to better understand the complexities of our lives, nature and the universe.

CHAPTER 2
Yin and Yang of Human Beings

Nothing on Earth is perfectly balanced in yin and yang, but of all God's creatures human beings are the most balanced, followed in decreasing order by all other animals, plants and, lastly, minerals. On an individual level, each person has his or her own unique variance of yin and yang resulting in different physical and mental characteristics. On the whole, however, people share more similarities than differences. According to the Human Genome Project and other recent studies, people are approximately 99.98% similar to one another and only 0.02% different. The degrees of yin-yang variance also fall into this 0.02% making the difference slight yet significant.

Yin Person, Yang Person

All people are born with a fundamental tilt of yin and yang. If divided into two groups the people who possess more yin than yang would be considered yin people and the people who possess more yang than yin would be considered yang people. The amount of yin and yang varies from person to person. Nevertheless, all yin people share common qualities associated with a predominance of yin and all yang people share common qualities associated with a predominance of yang.

God or Tao embodies the perfect balance of yin and yang and therefore suffers no illnesses and lives eternally. Human beings, on the other hand, struggle through life trying to maintain health because of their yin-yang variances. Regardless of what illness a person experiences, it is usually due to a fundamental imbalance of yin and yang. Yang persons have insufficient yin and an excess of yang. Yin persons have insufficient yang and an excess of yin.

It is possible to counter these imbalances through diet and lifestyle. It is not possible, however, for a yang person to transform into a yin person or vice versa. This is one limitation of being human.

Yin People

Yin gathers and materializes energy into substance. The external energetic activity of yin, however, appears weak. The physical and physiological characteristics of yin persons result from these factors. Yin persons have greater bone mass, more flesh and their physiological activities (such as blood circulation) are slower. As a result, they tend to be physically slow and cold and psychologically more passive and indecisive when compared to yang people.

Yin people exude elegance and calm. They are stable and tranquil, especially in the seated position. They speak prudently and cautiously, making efforts to hide their weaknesses and not make mistakes, particularly with people they meet for the first time. Their tendencies are often misinterpreted as cold-heartedness or indecision because they think too much. Yin persons dislike extreme situations. They try to remain passive, finding comfort in their present situation. At the same time, they continually compare themselves to others because of their insecurities. They feel anxious and apprehensive when they find themselves advancing ahead of the group.

Physically, yin persons tend to have big hips and narrow shoulders. Their weight is either average or heavy and they are generally big-boned. Their movements tend to be slow and their hands and feet cold. They dislike cold weather, so at home they usually close the windows and set their thermostats to higher temperatures. Ordinarily, yin persons like to drink warm water and eat hot soup. They also like warm colors such as red, orange or yellow to balance their "cold" constitutions.

Practitioners of eastern medicine analyze various physical features in order to gain a complete understanding of a person's yin-yang nature. Observation provides insight into the cause and proper treatment of various illnesses for each patient. Three primary areas of diagnosis are the patient's complexion, certain properties of the tongue–including color and coating–and the pulse. An eastern medical diagnosis of a yin person would most likely reveal a pale complexion, a tongue that lacks vitality and looks pale, and a weak pulse indicating low blood pressure.

YIN AND YANG OF HUMAN BEINGS

Yang People

Yang dissolves substance and transforms it into energy. Thus yang persons have less substance, manifesting in thin bones and a thin stature. The energetic action in their bodies is strong so their physiological activity is vigorous. They tend to have warmer bodies and swift physical movements.

Yang people have the opposite characteristics of yin people. Yang people have fast and light movements. They seem unsettled in the seated position, like a wobbling top that is about to fall, which is difficult to see because they rarely sit still for any extended period of time. They are constantly on the go and move swiftly from place to place.

Yang people are decisive. They feel frustrated around people whose judgments or movements are slow. They have enormous dreams and goals so they are continually dissatisfied with their present situation and may change jobs frequently. Yang persons generally like to lead people and dislike having others meddle in their affairs. They simply do not want any obstructions on the path to their goals. Yang people would not hesitate to go up to a complete stranger and tell them what they think. They are also not shy about their weaknesses and have no problem revealing their innermost selves to others. They are sympathetic and tolerant of mistakes made by others because they themselves frequently make mistakes.

Physically, yang persons tend to have stronger, wider shoulders and smaller, weaker hips. They generally have thinner bones and are thin even though they tend to eat a lot. Yang persons have warm hands and feet and cannot tolerate hot weather. They generally like to keep their windows at home open and set their thermostats at low temperatures. Yang persons prefer cold water and generally like to order raw salads rather than hot soups at restaurants. They prefer cooling colors, such as blue and indigo, instead of warmer colors.

An eastern medical examination of a yang person would reveal a reddish complexion, a red tongue and a strong pulse, which indicates a higher blood pressure.

Yin People	Yang People
Appear calm	Appear active
Pale complexion	Reddish complexion
Pale tongue	Reddish tongue
Deep and weak pulse	Superficial and stronger pulse
Weaker sound to the pulse beat when checking the blood pressure	Stronger sound to the pulse beat when checking the blood pressure
Narrow shoulders and wide hips	Wide shoulders and narrow hips
Colder hands	Warmer hands
Tends to set thermostat higher	Tends to set thermostat lower
Likes hot water in normal weather	Likes cold water in normal weather
Likes soup	Likes salad
Likes warmer colors, e.g., red and yellow	Likes cooler colors, e.g., blue and green
Walks slowly	Walks fast
Makes decisions slowly	Makes decisions quickly
Satisfied easily	Difficult to satisfy
Introverted	Extroverted
Dislikes meeting new people	Likes to meet new people

Table 2.1 Yin People vs. Yang People

Treatment for Yin People and Yang People

Yin persons can prevent and treat disease by eating more yang foods (see Chapter 5: Yin and Yang of Food and Diet) and by making efforts to develop a more broadminded and positive attitude towards life. They should also exercise more with a greater emphasis on rapid movements.

Yang persons can supplement their shortage of yin by eating more yin foods. They should also try to be realistic about life, discarding idle fantasies and grounding flighty emotions. Yang persons can also supplement their yin through meditation because it settles and quiets both the body and mind.

YIN AND YANG OF HUMAN BEINGS

Yin and Yang of Personalities

The personalities of yin and yang people coincide with a number of established personality theories including the Type A and Type B personality theory developed by Dr. Meyer Friedman and Dr. Ray H. Rosenman in the 1960s. According to Friedman and Rosenman, Type A personalities are goal driven, deadline setting workaholics. They are competitive multi-taskers whose sole focus is on outcome rather than process. They are sensitive and confrontational, and they speak and move quickly and frequently. Conversely, Type B personalities are more relaxed and easy-going. They tend to simply enjoy the process and take things in stride. They focus on the present moment and work methodically. They prioritize and delegate responsibilities. Needless to say, yang persons correspond to the Type A personality, while yin persons correspond to the Type B personality.

The Type A-Type B model was devised to research and explain the relationship between personality and heart disease. Compared to the yin-yang model, this theory is incomplete primarily because it ignores physical traits and focuses only on overt personality characteristics. This is one reason the theory was found a largely invalid indicator of heart disease.

Another personality theory that coincides with the yin-yang theory was developed by Carl Jung. Jung defined people as either Introverted or Extroverted and explained that these were congenital, instinctive traits.

The energetic tendencies of Extroverts extend outwards, so their personal identity is dependent upon feedback from the external world and other people. They are energetic, social, outgoing people who feel comfortable meeting new people and facing innovative challenges. They are aggressive, impulsive doers, movers and shakers who act first and think later. They focus more on the quantity or breadth of life experience rather than the quality and depth.

The energetic tendencies of Introverts extend inwards so they are more likely to focus on and appreciate their inner process. Introverts tend to be reflective and quiet and prefer solitude. They often feel uncomfortable in new situations or meeting new people so they prefer more intimate social situations. Introverts are idealists who dislike change. They consider all angles before acting and focus more on the quality and depth of life experience rather than the quantity or breadth.

Obviously, Extroverts are yang and Introverts are yin. However, because people possess both yin and yang traits, elements of the opposing personality find their way to the surface in certain situations.

Yin and Yang of Human Physiology

At the core of all of the body's physiological functions is a dynamic interplay of yin and yang. These two forces that support and define one another also transform into one another. When the yin or substantive aspects of the body transform into the yang or energetic aspects of the body, the process is called "energizing." This is what occurs when matter is converted into energy. The reciprocal process, energy (yang) converting into matter (yin), is known as "materialization." In the body the end product of materialization is cellular formation while the end product of the body's energizing function is muscle movement and glandular secretion. The constant interplay of these two functions is what we call life.

The materialization and energizing processes can be activated through the stimulation of the five senses. External stimuli, being either yin or yang in nature, are translated by the brain in terms of their relative strength and relative tilt of yin or yang. For example, the color red (fire/heat) is a yang stimulus, while the color blue (cold/water) is a yin stimulus. High-pitched, high frequency sounds are yang, and low-pitched, low frequency sounds are yin. Fragrant smells are yang and foul smells are yin. Flavors that are sweet, pungent or salty are yang, whereas bitter, sour or astringent flavors are yin. Pleasant, warm sensations, or pleasing sensations of pressure are yang, while rough, burning, stabbing, needle-like, abnormal sensations are all yin. Once the brain receives the stimuli, it analyzes the input and activates the appropriate energizing or materializing physiological action by sending orders to various parts of the body through the nervous and hormonal systems.

When the body requires more energy (yang) a command goes out to the sympathetic nervous system, which increases the secretion of hormones such as epinephrine, cortisone, thyroxin and testosterone. At the same time, the liver initiates the process of glycolysis. In glycolysis, glycogen (a byproduct of sugar) stored in the liver is converted into glucose and then supplied to muscle cells via the blood. Once in the muscle cells, glucose is transformed into its simplified state, called acetyl coenzyme A (acetyl CoA). CoA then enters the TCA cycle (citric acid cycle or tricarboxylic acid cycle or Krebs cycle) to create ATP, a rarified form of energy. ATP then stimulates muscular activity.

When the body needs more cells (yin), a command goes out to the parasympathetic nervous system, increasing the secretion of hormones such as insulin, growth hormone, parathyroid hormone, estrogen, progesterone and melatonin. Parasympathetic stimulation also stops the TCA cycle and stimulates glycogenesis. These processes create the fats and proteins necessary for cellular formation. The energizing and materialization processes are illustrated in the following diagram (Fig. 2.1).

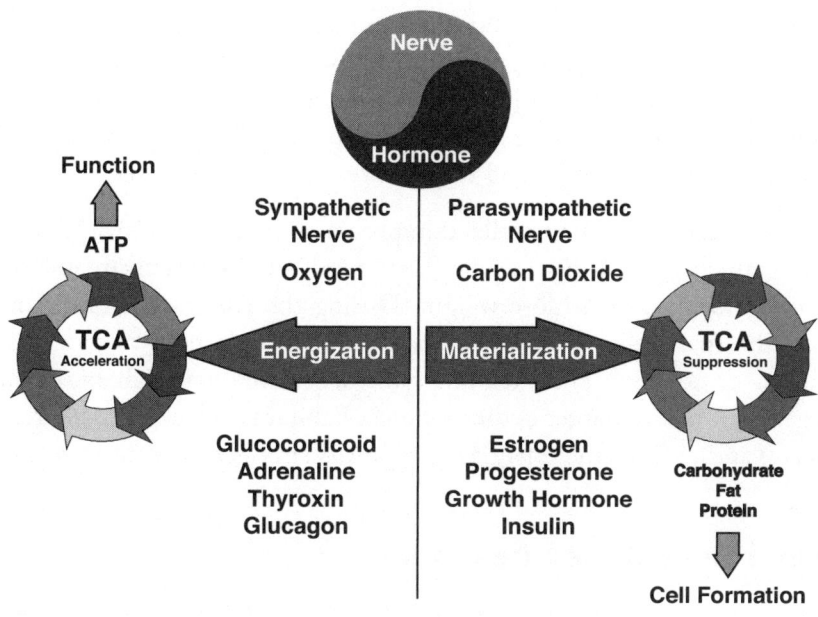

Figure 2.1 Yin-Yang of Human Physiology

During the day, when it is bright and noisy (yang), the materializing function is almost at a complete standstill, while the energizing function is in full swing. Sympathetic nerves are stimulated, cortisone is secreted, and muscles are active. The organs that lie above the diaphragm (a yang region) become excited. The heartbeat increases and blood pressure rises. Lung capacity and breathing rate also increase. Glycogen breakdown increases so that glucose and oxygen may be distributed to every cell. Inside the cells, the TCA cycle is hard at work creating ATP. Because of this energizing function, people are generally better suited to perform physical activities during the day.

At night (yin) when it is dark and quiet, the energizing function quiets down and the materializing function creeps into action. The parasympathetic nervous system is stimulated, and growth hormone and melatonin are secreted. Muscle movement and the heart rate are reduced, resulting in a decrease in lung function and a drop in blood pressure. This is why asthma attacks and neuralgic pain due to poor blood circulation worsens at night. Glycogenesis occurs and the TCA cycle slows down. Acetyl CoA is used to form protein and fats, which then form cells. New cells replace old ones, people gain weight, and children grow taller. This gives truth to the old eastern adage, "In order to grow taller, you must sleep a lot." In addition, the reproductive organs are in the domain of parasympathetic nerve distribution, so at night men get erections without external stimulation and women's sexual desire increases.

The energizing and materialization processes are also sensitive to seasonal and climate changes. Yang seasons (spring and summer) activate energizing actions so people tend to lose weight. During the yin seasons (autumn and winter) the materializing action is stronger so people tend to gain weight. Habitants of northern polar regions (yin), where the materializing action is stronger, tend to have larger bodies, whereas habitants of the southern, tropical regions (yang), where the energizing action is stronger, tend to have smaller bodies.

Yin and Yang of the Life Cycle

Some of the most advanced theories of quantum physics state that matter broken down into its smallest component is nothing more than vibrating energy. This means that the entire universe consists of only empty space. This theory coincides with the famous Buddhist statement: "Emptiness is color, and color is emptiness." Emptiness implies a vacuum or void, while color implies perceptible things with form or shape. When you translate this into yin and yang, comparing perceptible and imperceptible, color is yang and emptiness is yin. Yin is implicit. It is anything that has not yet manifested. Yang is explicit and anything that has already manifested. The human body comes from emptiness, becomes form, and then returns to emptiness. From yin, it becomes yang, and then returns to yin or, in other words, ashes to ashes and dust to dust.

According to traditional eastern medicine, infants are considered "bodies of pure yang," (although nothing really exists that is purely yang). The reason for this is that infants have rapid pulses, their bodies are shiny, and they give off a lot of heat–all yang traits. Human life begins as inorganic matter (yin) and progresses to its peak of yang at birth. As people age, they gradually move towards yin again. At approximately forty years of age, the phenomenon of materialization is clearly noticeable and becomes more pronounced with each advancing year. When a person dies, he or she returns to yin, to an inorganic state. From this perspective, sad though it may be, human beings begin dying the moment they are born.

Children and Elders

Comparing the dispositions of children and seniors clearly illustrates the differences between yin and yang. Children are very active, while seniors move much less frequently and more slowly. Children speak quickly with little regard to what they are saying, while elderly people generally speak more slowly and thoughtfully. In addition, children are generally more comfortable in cold weather and are not as averse to eating cold foods as are the elderly. Because children have a lot of yang, they are lacking in yin. Elderly people, on the other hand, have plenty of yin so their yang is lacking. Because of these attributes, eastern medicine often bases its diagnoses of children on syndromes arising from insufficient yin while elderly people are diagnosed based on syndromes that result from a lack of yang. According to eastern medicine, children are advised to eat foods and herbs rich in yin and elderly people are advised to eat foods and herbs that are rich in yang.

Yin and Yang of a Mid-life Crisis

At forty, men and women's transformation towards yin and away from the "pure yang" into which they were born, becomes profound and results in significant mental and physical changes. This is commonly known as a mid-life crisis and is primarily caused by hormonal changes.

Testosterone is responsible for masculine traits. When its levels are high, men are more yang in nature. They are louder, more boastful and more active. They can also be more broad minded and thus more tolerant. Heightened yang energy can be likened to having more firepower, giving its owner more courage. Yang energy expands outward affecting other people, situations and conditions. Yin energy contracts, withdraws and generally leads to a more narrow focus.

After forty, as male hormonal secretions dwindle, men become more practical and narrow-minded as their yin (contracting) energy grows and their yang (expanding) energy dissipates. As a result, men's yin characteristics become more prominent. They begin to question the power that yang had over their lives. Little things begin to bother them and they start meddling in the trivialities of home life. Their ideas of taking over the world transform into simply seeing the world from a more relaxed perspective. Rather than being an active participant, they become passive observers from the sidelines.

Feminine traits are due in large part to the secretion of female hormones, such as estrogen and progesterone. After forty there is a reduction in the secretion of female hormones and women's yang characteristics become more prominent. They become more broadminded and socially active because their male hormones are more prominent; their yang energy is less hindered by the presence of female, yin hormones. Hence, they become more yang, or active.

During a mid-life crisis as men's masculinity and women's femininity decline, they may develop feelings of emptiness or depression. One way for men and women to endure this crisis is to gain a deeper understanding of the reason for their changing states (and that of their partner or spouse) using the theory of yin and yang as a guide.

These changes are part of the natural cycle of life. However, because the state of adulthood is one of relative stability compared to childhood or adolescence, when hormonal changes occur later in life it is often difficult to cope with the sudden change. The best way to weather the storm is to maintain perspective and attempt to restore balance by supplementing the waning yin or yang energy.

Eastern medicine considers hormonal changes to be a decline of "Jing" or

"Essence," the substance from which all of the body's energy is derived. (Jing will be more fully discussed in Chapters 3 and 13.) To help build Jing, eastern medicine ascribes to enacting certain diet and lifestyle modifications as well as taking supplements and herbal remedies and performing exercises targeting hormonal health and spiritual clarity.

Later chapters discuss many of these solutions. In addition, doctors and acupuncturists trained in eastern medicine are good sources of information and guidance. Acupuncture has been shown to help balance hormones and maintain health and many eastern herbal formulas are available to restore balance to the system.

Mental and spiritual cultivations through meditation, prayer, and mind-body exercises such as Tai Chi, Qigong and Yoga are very important to help balance yin and yang energies. They also promote the intuition and awareness necessary to maintain a broader perspective of life's natural cycles.

Easterners and Westerners

Another way to illustrate the yin-yang variations among people is to look at the differences between Easterners and Westerners. Although generalizations are ultimately stereotypical, there is always some element of truth to them. Keep in mind that when we say "an Easterner is like this," or "a Westerner is like that," we do not mean that all Easterners or Westerners fit the stereotype; we are simply pointing out general tendencies.

If we look at physical activity we find that, on the whole, Westerners tend to be more active (yang) than Easterners. Their facial expressions change frequently and their movements tend to be rapid. Easterners, on the other hand, tend to have slower, more subtle ways of expressing themselves and slower physical movements because they tend to be more yin. The difference between the two is demonstrated in the expressions they show when they are treated unkindly by others: Westerners will grimace, frown, and generally appear upset, whereas Easterners will tend to mask their expressions. Remember, yin persons possess a greater materializing function that causes a reduction in energy consumption. This, in turn, slows down physiological functioning, such as that of facial expressions.

In Korean "Jum Jahn Ta" is translated as "gentle." Its literal translation is "not young." In the East, elders (yin) are given a great deal of respect. So Easterners tend to increase their age when asked how old they are. In the West, things are just the opposite; people always want to be perceived as younger (more yang). They dislike being thought of as "old" and often times assign a negative connotation to it. There is an incredible amount of money spent every year on cosmetic surgeries and beauty products in America. People fear becoming old because of the social stigma attached to the aging process. Youth implies activity (yang) while age implies slowing down (yin).

Statistics show that Westerners' heads are roughly one-eighth the size of their bodies. Easterners, on the other hand, tend to have heads that are roughly one-seventh the size of their bodies. According to eastern physiognomy,[1] a person with a smaller head in proportion to his or her body tends to think more practically, and as a result, tends to make decisions and execute ideas quickly. A person with a larger head proportion, on the other hand, tends to be idealistic, indecisive and is less likely to execute ideas. Thus, according to eastern physiognomy and the Form-Function Principle that smaller things move faster, Westerners have a more yang-type brain functioning and Easterners have a more yin-type brain functioning.

We can also see these yin-yang characteristics in the everyday activities of these two groups of people. The saws that Westerners use to cut wood are designed to cut only during the pushing stroke. Eastern saws, in contrast, are designed to cut only during the pulling stroke. When Westerners sweep the floor, they typically sweep dust away from their bodies. Easterners tend to sweep dust towards their bodies. The reason for these seemingly insignificant habits is simple: since Westerners are yang, their pushing force is more developed. They are, therefore, more comfortable pushing things away from their bodies. The opposite is true of Easterners. Since they are yin, their pulling force is more developed. They are, therefore, more likely to pull things towards their bodies.

The pushing-pulling contrast is also evident in social behaviors. Westerners tend to be more extroverted and sociable ("pushing out of their shells"), while Easterners tend to be more introverted and timid ("pulling into their shells"). When a person is bashful there is a tendency to contract the body as energy is gathered inwards.

When eating soup Easterners usually tilt the bowl towards their bodies (yin) and spoon the soup toward their bodies, while Westerners tilt the bowl away from their bodies and initially spoon soup away from them (yang) before bringing it back to their mouths. The utensils used while eating also demonstrate a yin-yang contrast. In the West, meals are generally eaten with a knife and fork. These utensils are dissimilar to one another and thus independent and solitary pieces. They are also generally made of metal and are therefore more yang in nature. The chopsticks generally used by Easterners are only effective in pairs, often made of bamboo or wood, and they do not cut or penetrate the food. These qualities are yin in nature.

Because Westerners are generally more yang than Easterners, they have a lot of heat in their bodies and are more comfortable in a cool environment. When Easterners (who have relatively less heat) go into an air-conditioned room where Westerners are gathered in the summertime, they feel very cold. Often Easterners who work with Westerners must wear sweaters while working indoors in the summer. Having a lot of heat implies that substance is rapidly changing into energy, a yang phenomenon.

There are many more examples of this yin-yang dichotomy. When calling someone to them Easterners will make a hand motion with their palms down (yin) whereas the Westerners will make the same hand motion with their palms up (yang). This may sound funny, but in the East a palm up motion is usually reserved for calling dogs. When ringing a large bell, Easterners will hit it with a wooden pole from outside (exterior to interior: yin motion) while the Westerners will strike it from inside with a rope (interior to exterior: yang motion).

One of the most noticeable differences between these two groups is where people choose to sit. In the West most people sit on a chair whether at home, out dining, or at work. But in the East, though customs have changed quite a bit due to western influence, most people sit with a cushion on the floor. Sitting on a chair is more yang due to its proximity to the heavens (yang) while sitting on the floor is more yin due to its proximity to the ground (yin). One possible reason for this difference is that a Heavenly Father or God (yang) figure traditionally dominated western culture, while Mother Nature (yin) was more revered in the East.

While Westerners have always worn black (yin) to funerals, traditional eastern mourning clothes were white (yang). In the East death is considered a return to the source. Life and death are seen as two sides of the same coin, or as a circular path with the soul being reincarnated or transmigrated again and again. White is considered the color of life and enlightenment. It is the base from which all other colors issue forth, like a blank canvas prior to any great work of art. Thus, from this life with its wide array of colors, at death a person returns to the original source in order to be able to start life anew.

Nowadays, black is worn at funerals in both the East and the West. Black has been associated with the yin qualities of darkness and death for eons. Black matches the solemn atmosphere (yin) of the funeral.

Conclusion

Yin and yang allow us a vantage point from which we can clearly see what distinguishes one person from another. They provide us a platform from which we can differentiate ourselves from others based on our innate attributes, psychological tendencies, physical differences and personal leanings. They also function as a personal guide to the human condition, giving us insight into what we can do to establish balance within ourselves and harmony in our relationships. Yin and yang allow us to appreciate the intricacies and delicate balance that is the human race without judgment or prejudice because it reminds us that our differences exist so that we may exist.

CHAPTER 3
Yin and Yang of Sex

Without a doubt sex is one of the most important parts of our lives. It can impact our lives positively or negatively in many ways—mentally, emotionally and physically. By applying yin-yang theory to sex, we can gain a greater understanding of it that enhances our lives. One important way in which yin-yang theory looks at sex is from the perspective of the energetic exchange that occurs during the act. From this perspective, sexual activity can be objectively seen as strengthening or weakening a person. It can either give a person vibrant health and longevity or poor health and premature death. Before we can look at sex, though, it is important to understand the inherent sexual differences between men and women in terms of yin and yang.

Yin and Yang of Men and Women

What makes men and women different—genetics, hormones, social influences? While these do play important roles, applying yin-yang theory to gender differences reveals a more general distinction.

Relatively speaking, men are yang and women are yin. Yang is an ascending, outward moving, expansive energy reflected in the physical and psychological characteristics men embody. Yin is a descending, inward moving, contracting force reflected in the physical and emotional manifestations of women.

Physically, men typically have more well-developed upper bodies and shoulders while women generally have more developed lower bodies and hips. Men tend to be physically larger, stronger and faster and have more body hair—all yang traits. Since men are more yang, they also burn more energy, generate greater amounts of body heat and perspire more than women while performing the same amount of work.[1]

Women tend to be physically smaller, slower and weaker then men, with less body hair. Women have the ability to procreate life and tend to live longer than men. Their longevity results from their superior ability to conserve energy and delay the breakdown or degeneration of their bodies.[2] As they store more fat cells (yin) in their bodies, they also have softer skin. These are all yin traits.

Psychologically and behaviorally, men tend to be more aggressive and reckless (yang) and women more cautious, patient and polite (yin). Men are more extroverted, competitive, dogmatic, self-righteous and resolute, while women are more introverted, passive, cooperative, gentle, docile, empathetic, caring and indecisive. Men tend to rely on logic and reason, while women find it easier to rely on their intuition and emotions. Men are louder and display their emotions more readily, while women are quieter and more apt to hide their emotions. Nevertheless, in our society the emotions men display are more yang in nature like anger and pride, whereas women are usually quite comfortable showing more yin emotions such as acceptance and sadness or even jealousy. On the whole, as extreme yin always turns into yang, women are more talkative and sentimental than men.

The following yin-yang diagram illustrates the physical and psychological differences between men and women (Fig. 3.1).

Figure 3.1 Yin-Yang of Men and Women

YIN AND YANG OF SEX

This diagram represents the relative size of the head in relation to the reproductive area of the body. The male symbol places emphasis on the upper (head) region (the rounded aspect) while the female symbol emphasizes the lower (uterine) region. Eastern traditions assign psychological attributes to these physical differences. In the East, it is said that "men think with their heads and women think with their uteruses," meaning that men are more rational and logical (yang) and women have greater intuitive (yin) abilities.

The yin and yang distinctions between men and women also come into play when looking at the shape of the genitals and the nature of sexual intercourse. Men's genitals protrude outward while women's genitals are more "contracted" into the body. When sexually aroused, men get an erection. Expansion is yang in nature, and an erection of the male genitals is considered to be the epitome of yang expression. For men, obtaining an erection is a relatively rapid process, as is the attainment of an orgasm and the subsequent diminished desire for additional sexual activity. As yang is swift, these actions are consistent with men's yang nature. Men's diminished desire in sex after ejaculation is due to the principle of extreme yang converting into yin. Women tend to be slower to achieve excitation, which is followed by longer orgasms and slower settling. Slow changes are yin.

During sex men often enjoy vigorous motion, while women receive pleasure from slower, more fluid movements. Women frequently move in response to their partner, making them more yin. Additionally, women often close their eyes during sex to enhance the feeling of pleasure. With their eyes closed their focus is more internal and thus more yin. Women are known to be more vocal during sex than men. When women are very sexually aroused, yin is in the extreme. Following the principle of Mutual Transformation, when yin is in the extreme, it converts into yang and the yang energy rises up to the throat to escape as cries of passion.

It is interesting to note that there exists an intimate relationship between sounds made during sex and the energy of the internal organs. Eastern medical theory states that the Kidneys are the most yin organs in the body because they are dark in color and sit low in the abdomen. The Kidneys are also in charge of all sexual activity. Moaning is the most yin sound a person can make. It is low and comes from deep within. During sex, when the activity of the

Kidneys is at its zenith, people moan. The Heart, on the other hand, is the most yang organ because it is situated high in the body and it is red. Its major functions are to regulate mental activities, emotions and blood circulation. Laughter is the most yang sound as it is high pitched and generally comes from the chest. When the heart is healthy and happy, laughter occurs.

The relationship between the Heart and the Kidneys is an interplay between yin and yang. Although sex is governed by the Kidneys, the Heart plays an important role as it controls the mind, emotions and the circulation of blood to the sex organs. When the body is in balance the Heart and the Kidneys are in harmony. This will lead to abundant sexual energy and pleasurable sexual experiences.

The Infinitely Divisible (Wo)Man

Although men are ultimately more yang and women more yin, the relationship between yin and yang always adheres to the Six Basic Principles.

The principle of Infinite Divisibility states that nothing is ever purely yang or purely yin. This includes the attributes of men and women. Men possess certain physical characteristics that are yin when compared to women. For example, Men's chests are generally flatter (more yin) than women. They also have thicker skin and hair and their voices generally resonate at a lower frequency.

Women, on the other hand possess physical traits that are yang compared to men. For instance, women have a pain threshold seven times that of men (which is helpful in childbirth). Research also indicates that women have a slightly higher resting pulse rate than men. Women also have a greater number of neurons connecting the two hemispheres of the brain, allowing them to multitask more effectively.

We can also see the principle of Infinite Divisibility at play in men and women's psychological and emotional attributes. When problem solving, women generally take a more broad or "collective" (yang) perspective, while men analyze situations more narrowly and linearly (yin). Women are generally stronger and more resolute once they have made up their minds to accomplish a task. The single working mother is a good example of the emotional strength women possess. We often see this in older couples. Men live an average of two years after their wives pass; women, however, usually live much longer after the death of a mate.

Another way we see Infinite Divisibility at work is in the characterization of men and women as wholly more yin or more yang. Women (yin) can be classified as yin women or yang women (women with more yang attributes and tendencies). Men (yang) can also be subdivided into yang men or yin men, depending on their natures.

There are a number of ways to determine the yin or yang nature of men and women strictly by their physical appearance. Dark colors are indicative of yin energy because they are seen as more "inactive" and "quiet." Thus, darker skin and hair are considered to be more yin qualities.

Thick and elastic lips are considered yin. Lips are part of the lowest (yin) orifice and sense organ of the face and so are considered yin. Their thickness indicates an abundance of yin energy in the yin region of the face.

Eyes are considered yang because they are the brightest, most active, highest sense organ on the face. They reveal the state of yang energy in the body. People with strong yang energy tend to have reflective, brilliant, penetrating eyes in contrast to those who have less yang (or greater yin) energy, who tend to have "sleepy" eyes.

According to western stereotypes blondes are typically thought to be sexy. However, this stereotype may not be true when applying yin-yang theory to hair color. The head is the highest point on the body and is, therefore, the location where yang reaches its extreme. Following the principle of Mutual Transformation, once yang reaches its extreme, it transforms into yin. So anything that grows from this region–hair–is considered to be yin. As the nature of yin is dark, the darker a person's hair color, the more yin (and thus sexy) the person according to yin-yang theory.

The following table indicates general yin and yang distinctions of various parts of our bodies (Table 3.1).

	Yin	**Yang**
Shoulders	narrow	wide
Hips	wide	narrow
Abdomen	protruding	flat
Head Hair	dark, thick	light, thin
Body Hair	less	more
Skin	dark	light
Head Size	smaller	larger
Lips	thick	thin
Eyes	sleepy	penetrating, sparkling

Table 3.1 Yin-Yang of Physical Characteristics

The following are descriptions and examples of (1) yin woman, (2) yang woman, (3) yin man and (4) yang man.

(1) The Classic Yin Woman:
- Hair: brown or black
- Eyes: sleepy and seductive
- Lips: thick
- Skin: dark and soft
- Hips: wide
- Personality: quiet, refined, soft spoken, secretive, seductive
- Examples: Marilyn Monroe, Gina Lollobrigida, Sophia Loren, Catherine Zeta Jones, Angelina Jolie, Penelope Cruz, Cleopatra, Elizabeth Taylor

(2) The Classic Yang Woman:
- Hair: blonde or red
- Eyes: sharp, reflective, sparkling
- Lips: thin
- Skin: fair/light colored and delicate
- Hips: narrow

- Shoulders: relatively wide
- Personality: outgoing, cheerful, bright, talkative, social, tomboy
- Examples: Madonna, Jennifer Aniston, Gwen Stefani, Pamela Anderson, Jessica Simpson, Sarah Jessica Parker

(3) The Classic Yin Man:

- Hair: thick, dark hair
- Eyes: sleepy
- Lips: thick
- Skin: dark or rough
- Hips: fairly large hips (for a man)
- Shoulders: relatively narrow
- Abdomen: protruding lower abdomen (yin region)
- Personality: somewhat dull and tactless nature
- Examples: Antonio Banderas, George Clooney, Robert Downey, Jr., Russell Crow, Johnny Depp

(4) The Classic Yang Man:

- Head: large
- Hair: thin or bald
- Eyes: sharp, reflective
- Lips: thin
- Skin: fair
- Hips: small
- Shoulders: wide
- Personality: quick to take action, sensitive, rash, reckless, or foolhardy
- Examples: Brad Pitt, Arnold Schwarzenegger, Dolph Lundgren, Fabio, Clint Eastwood, Sting

Source Qi

Eastern medical doctrines refer to the energies of the body as "Qi" (pronounced 'chee'). Qi initiates, activates, catalyzes and supports every thought, action, emotion and function of the body. There are a number of different types of Qi involved in these activities.

Gu Qi or *Grain Qi* is the energy derived from food. *Wei Qi*, or *Protective Qi* generally circulates on the surface of the body and is responsible for protecting the body from pathogens and initiating the inflammatory response. *Source Qi* is inherited from the mother during pregnancy and from both parents at the time of conception. Its main role is to maintain balance or homeostasis in the body by managing influences from the surrounding environment. It regulates the yin and yang of all physiological processes and the programming of DNA. It is also the type of Qi involved in sex.

Source Qi is like a car battery; while it is continually recharged by *Grain Qi*, it is also constantly used to fuel the physiological processes of the body, including sexual intercourse. Although a car battery can be replaced when it no longer holds a charge, once a person's *Source Qi* is exhausted, he or she dies because there is no longer sufficient energy to maintain a proper balance of yin and yang in the body.

Some people are born with a shortage of *Source Qi* and get sick easily. For most others, as *Source Qi* is depleted by old age, their susceptibility to illness increases. When *Source Qi* is lacking, the controls of the body become weak and the balance of yin and yang is lost. This is the reason a person dies when *Source Qi* is used up. While we inherit *Source Qi* from our parents, it must be maintained with a healthy lifestyle in order to achieve longevity.

The *I Ching* states that the universe was created out of the interplay of two opposing forces: *expansion*, embodied by the "Big Bang" (yang), and *contraction*, embodied by a "Black Hole" (yin). Human beings are created in much the same way. When men and women are separated, yin and yang are divided. Through intercourse the same forces of expansion and contraction are invoked and a universe (Tai Chi) is created (Fig. 3.2).

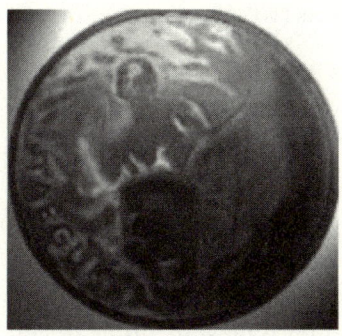

Figure 3.2 Tai Chi of a Man and a Woman

During intercourse the yang elements, such as increased heart and respiratory rates and an elevated state of excitement, are manifestations of expansive energy. When men reach orgasm the process of expansion is reversed with the ejaculation of semen, a yin substance. At the same time, the woman's uterus contracts and absorbs the semen along with the energy surrounding the semen. If an egg is fertilized, 270 days later a new universe is created with the birth of a baby.

The interplay of yin and yang during sex highlights the significance of the energetic exchange that occurs. For this reason, it is important for men and women to understand the dangers of engaging in frequent sexual activity with an improper partner and the benefits that can be derived from sex with a partner who is an energetic match.

Yin and Yang of Sex

A great deal of energy is exchanged between two people engaging in sexual activity. Orgasms release *Source Qi* from the body. The release and absorption of *Source Qi* can make a person stronger or weaker depending on his or her partner.

Yin women take longer to warm up and attain orgasm and their climaxes last a long time. Because the nature of women is predominantly yin, yin women are particularly adept at absorbing energy; they are also particularly attractive in a dark and seductive way. Yin also represents reproductive capabilities, so strong yin women tend to carry their pregnancies well and have strong children.

Yang men are predominantly yang and so are easily aroused, quickly attain orgasm and readily release great quantities of their *Source Qi*. Yang-natured men who frequently engage in sexual activities with yin-natured women would be risking their health. As the man released his *Source Qi*, the yin woman would be able to absorb her partner's energy. Because of her strong absorptive force she would also reclaim a majority of her own. So as she grew stronger from this relationship, he would grow weaker. Ultimately, his immune system may weaken and he could become susceptible to catching colds or developing allergies.

Sex manuals in the East expound on the importance of identifying a strong yin woman. A woman of this nature is known as "a woman beautiful enough to cause the downfall of a country," because she could extract the *Source Qi* of any ruler that fell under her spell. This is akin to the story of Helen of Troy or Cleopatra who dismantled able bodied rulers with their womanly ways.

The strong yin man would not suffer much loss of *Source Qi* even if he were to have sex with a strong yin woman. Upon ejaculation he would release less *Source Qi* (because of the strong absorptive power of yin), and some of the *Source Qi* released would be reabsorbed.

Men born with strong yin energy are actually able to absorb the *Source Qi* of women. If this type of man frequently has sex with a woman with strong yang energy, there is the danger that she may lose a lot of her *Source Qi* and become ill. She could become thin and emaciated, with dark circles under her eyes and an increased tendency for illness.

Like a strong yang man, a strong yang woman will tend to get sexually excited and orgasm quickly, scattering her *Source Qi*, unable to reabsorb it. This type of woman would benefit by meditating and eating foods, such as many types of sea food, and taking herbs, such as rehmannia root, that nourish the body's yin energy. (See Chapter 13 for additional information.) There are also sexual positions mentioned in the ancient eastern manual *Plain Girl* that prolong sexual excitement and orgasm, allowing the *Source Qi* to be reabsorbed.

The strong yin man, on the other hand, should take herbs that tonify yang, such as ginseng, and make an effort to ejaculate faster. This way he can release and return the *Source Qi* that he absorbs from his partner.

A strong yang man should attempt to cultivate his yin energy through meditation and ingesting yin-nourishing herbs and foods. He should also follow the recommendations given in *Plain Girl* to avoid injury to his *Source Qi*. The strong yin woman, meanwhile, should ingest herbs that are yang in nature. She should also exercise in order to strengthen her yang energy. This way she will experience quicker and more frequent orgasms, releasing a portion of the *Source Qi* she has been accumulating.

Fortunately, the yang man has an appropriate partner in the strong yang woman. This woman shares the same characteristics as the strong yang man. As previously mentioned, she has a fair skin, a large head, thin hair, sharp eyes, narrow hips, swiftness and sensitivity. She, like her counterpart, will attain orgasm quickly. However, she will not be able to absorb most of the *Source Qi* released by the man; thus a portion of it will be returned to him. When a strong yang man has sex with a strong yang woman, he will feel that his orgasm is relatively slow and will release less of his *Source Qi*.

Health, Longevity and Enlightenment

The cultivation of *Source Qi* is the path to health, longevity and enlightenment. In the past wealthy men of the East (mostly nobles and businessmen) bought concubines in order to maintain their health and increase their longevity. The steward of the household, well versed in the principle of yin and yang, would make the purchase. He would examine the prospective woman's physiognomy and translate it into yin and yang. If she were a strong yang woman, with the ability to readily release her *Source Qi*, then she was purchased.

There are also women who use sex to "recharge their batteries." It is actually easier for women to do so because they are yin by nature and have the inborn capacity to absorb *Source Qi*. After all, copulation and fertilization require that women "absorb" the male *Source Qi* (sperm) into their uterus. Although they may be well over forty, they maintain the beauty and skin of much younger women by frequently having sex with young men. Since younger men are more yang, they easily release their *Source Qi* for these women to absorb.

There exist masters in the East who, through training, meditation and ingesting herbs, have learned to move their *Source Qi* at will. These masters, trained in the art of supplementing their *Source Qi* through sex, will generally attempt to attract women with strong yang energy. These men bring women to orgasm quickly in order to absorb the *Source Qi* that is released. Once they absorb their partner's *Source Qi*, they quickly leave to meditate and transform their newly acquired energy into their own *Source Qi*. Unfortunately, intentionally stealing another person's *Source Qi* is both troublesome and unethical and thereby a hindrance to reaching enlightenment.

(For additional information on cultivating *Source Qi*, please refer to Chapter 13: Yin and Yang of Performance Enhancing Drugs.)

Koong Hap

To prevent an imbalance of yin or yang in a relationship, couples in Korea have a *Koong Hap* done on them prior to marriage. *Koong Hap* is a prediction of marital harmony performed by a fortuneteller with an in-depth understanding of yin-yang principles. *Koong* refers to the uterus or the reproductive organs, while *Hap* implies the act of checking the fit, or suitability, of two things. Thus, *Koong Hap* implies checking to see whether or not the reproductive organs of a couple are compatible.

Traditionally, it was not possible to know whether a couple would be able to have orgasms at the same time before marriage. *Koong Hap* would check the horoscopes of both partners for compatibility. One aspect of *Koong Hap* involves looking at the body shape of each partner. If the upper body is relatively more developed, that person is yang, and vice versa. Through this simple observation, one can determine whether both members of the couple shared the same energy (yin or yang) or not. If the yin and yang of a couple were in complete opposition, the results were not favorable and the couple was deemed incompatible. Knowing the *Koong Hap* before marriage, therefore, was an important precautionary measure. It was used to prevent illness and premature death due to loss of *Source Qi* during sex. Of course, in modern times there is a great deal more premarital sex, during which two partners can determine their own sexual compatibility. Nevertheless, the more astrological aspects of *Koong Hap* are still widely practiced, perhaps as a way of maintaining cultural tradition.

Southern Man, Northern Woman

In Korea, "Southern man and Northern woman" is a saying that implies men from southern regions and women from northern regions are more masculine and feminine, respectively, than men and women from other regions. Because southern regions have more sunlight, they are brighter and thus infused with more yang energy. This results in the people living there being more yang. People living in southern climates are thought to be more active, open-minded and romantic. As men are by nature yang, southern men are seen as the epitome of masculine yang energy. Northern regions, on the other hand, have less sunlight and thus less yang energy. In comparison to southern regions, northern regions are yin. The relative abundance of yin energy makes the people living there more yin. Thus, people of northern climates are thought to be more passive, introspective, and less social. As women are yin, northern women are viewed as particularly yin or feminine.

Based on this yin-yang perspective, southern men tend to be more active, social, and are generally more popular with women. Meanwhile, northern women tend to be more quiet, passive, gentle, shy and feminine, implicitly attracting the attention of men. Although this may seem a radical concept, it is supported by some observations that we tend to take for granted in the West.

For instance, on an international scale, cultural icons of romance in the western world are often from southern climates. Don Juan and Carlos Casanova are both "Latin lovers" from Spain and Italy. In contrast, it is hard for us to conceive of an "Arctic lover;" the cold northern climates call to mind images of snow and ice rather than burning passion.

The nature of yin and yang, which men and women possess, is the major determining factor in sexual attraction or repulsion. People with similar characteristics are often attracted to one another while those who are strongly dissimilar would not want to be near one another. While it is true that "opposites attract," this only happens when the differences are slight. Men and women who are extremely different would be unable to circumvent those opposing characteristics to develop harmony in their relationship.

CHAPTER 4
Yin and Yang of the Brain

In her remarkable personal account Jill Bolte Taylor, a brain scientist and researcher, tells what it is like to survive a massive stroke of the brain's left-hemisphere.[1] According to Taylor, as her left hemisphere repeatedly went "off line" during the stroke, she oscillated between having the cognitive awareness and abilities the left hemisphere provides and moving into an uncharted realm where she could not distinguish herself from objects around her or communicate in a language others would understand. Her extraordinary experience boldly illustrates the fact that the two hemispheres of the human brain control completely separate functions of human activity.

The insight Taylor provides us into the inner workings of the brain aptly demonstrates how everything in the universe, including the human brain, is made up of two opposing forces. By recognizing yin and yang aspects of various parts of the brain, we reach a more complete understanding of the brain's complexities.

Two Hemispheres of the Brain

The left hemisphere is considered yang, since it is in charge of language and calculations and because the speed at which this hemisphere processes information is relatively fast. The left hemisphere is also in charge of logic, reason, analysis and digital interpretations, and its strength is in synthesizing objective data. Linear, rational thought and objective reasoning are considered yang because they are more rapid, concrete and direct processes.

The right hemisphere is considered yin because it is in charge of artistic talents and intuition, which occur at a slower rate. Creativity may appear spontaneous, but intuition and inspiration require a great deal of self actualization—a lengthy process—and true works of art involve great deliberation, study and planning before they materialize. The right hemisphere also controls the brain's analog processing as well as symbolic interpretations. Subjectivity, intuition and non-linear thoughts are yin processes.

Following is a chart of the Yin-Yang distinctions of the brain (Table 4.1).

Left Hemisphere (Yang)	Right Hemisphere (Yin)
Mathematics	Art
Language	Symbols
Science	Music
Logic	Emotion
Reason	Intuition
Analytical	Holistic
Digital	Analog
Information	Inference
Concrete/Objective	Associative/Subjective
Linear	Geometrical

Table 4.1 Yin-Yang of Brain Hemispheres

The yin and yang distinctions between the two hemispheres illustrate the brain's opposing forces. However, in a well-functioning brain the two hemispheres communicate through the corpus callosum, demonstrating the Mutual Dependence of yin and yang.

Front Brain - Hind Brain

Yin-yang theory considers dynamic activity and evolutionarily advanced functions to be yang. Therefore, when the brain is divided into its front and rear components, the front half is considered yang and the back half is considered yin (Table 4.2). The front of the brain contains the motor cortex, which is in charge of physical activities (yang). It also contains the evolutionarily newer (yang) part of the brain, the cerebral cortex, which is in charge of more evolved functions (yang), such as reasoning and judgment.

The hind brain is in charge of sensory reception, which is considered a yin activity because it is the act of gathering information. Following the principle of Mutual Consumption and Support, this sensory reception (yin) is stronger when all muscular activity (yang) has ceased. The hind brain also contains the cerebellum, the evolutionarily older (yin) part of the brain that is responsible for more primitive (yin) functions, such as reflex and balance (Fig. 4.1). These functions are considered yin because they are more innate and physical in nature.

Yang	Yin
Anterior Cortex	Posterior Cortex
Motor Movement	Sensory Reception
Cerebrum	Cerebellum

Table 4.2 Yin-Yang Regions of the Brain

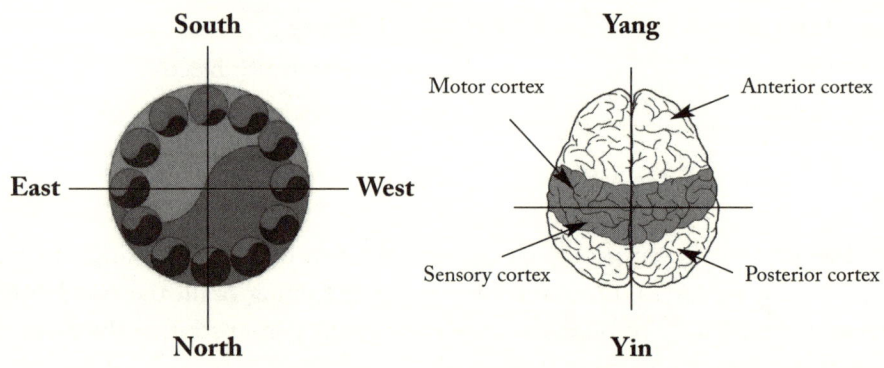

Figure 4.1 Yin-Yang Regions of the Brain

Memory and Sensation

The brain is in charge of both memory and sensation. Technically, memory is the storing of information. Because it is a gathering or contracting action, memory is considered a yin process. The hippocampus, which stores memories, is located in a yin region of the brain in deep folds of the temporal lobe.

Applying the principle of Infinite Divisibility to memory gives us a more accurate picture of this process. There are two distinct types of memory: short term and long term. As the name implies, short term memory (also called "active memory") is transient (yang). It holds small amounts of information for short periods of time and is rapidly accessed, all yang characteristics. Long term memories, on the other hand, are more slowly (yin) retrieved. The brain holds large quantities of these memories for long periods of time. Structural and functional changes to neural pathways occur in order to store this information. For all of these reasons, long term memory is considered yin.

The sensations of the body can be mapped out on a homunculus. A homunculus is a map of the motor and sensory zones of the human body imposed onto the brain (Fig. 4.2). This map conforms to the principles of yin and yang. The face and hands are located in the upper part of the body and are more mobile (yang). Their zones are in the outermost regions of the brain (yang). The legs and sexual organs are situated in the lower part of the body and are less mobile (yin). Their zones are folded into the brain (yin). The trunk, which is more yin than the arms and legs, is also folded inward at the bottom.

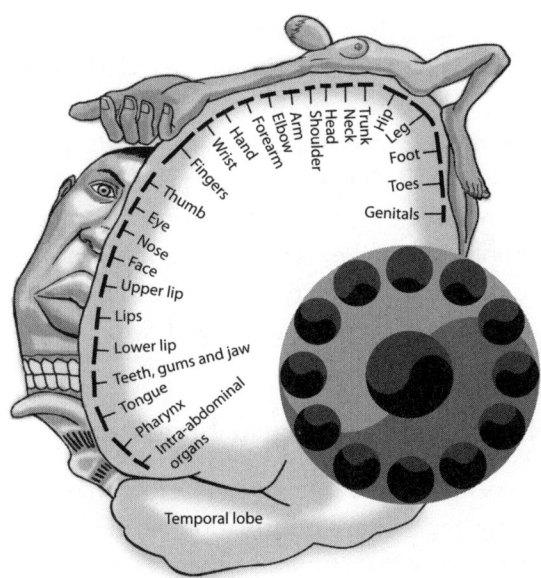

Figure 4.2 Homunculus

Yin and Yang of Sense Organs

One of the major tasks of the brain is sensory perception. Our senses give flavor and color to life and protect us from harm. These sense organs, like all other things, can be distinguished by their yin and yang characteristics.

The sense organs on the face (eyes, ears, nose and mouth) can be analyzed by their position, function, movement and workload. When looking at their location, the eyes and ears are considered yang organs because they are situated on the upper part of the face. Additionally, the information they receive arrives as sound waves and light frequencies, both elemental (yang) stimuli. The nose and mouth sit lower on the face (yin) and receive input in the form of molecules and substances (yin).

These sensory stimuli can be further broken down. Light moves more rapidly than sound waves and is therefore more yang. The molecules of odors are larger and move more slowly than either light or sound but are smaller than substances required to stimulate taste. Therefore, in terms of speed and weight, light is the most yang, followed in decreasing order by sound, odors and flavors.

In terms of movement, the eyes and mouth are more active (yang) than the nose and ears. The eyes constantly blink and the mouth opens and closes during many activities such as eating, speaking and at times breathing. The nose and ears, on the other hand, move infrequently if at all. In regard to workload, however, the Inversion Principle comes into play. Because the eyes and mouth have the ability to open and close, there is a significant amount of time, while sleeping, for example, when they are at rest and do not take in any stimuli, making them more yin in this regard. The nose and ears, on the other hand, are always open and do not have a mechanism with which they can escape stimuli, making them more yang in this sense.

The Polar Nature of Vision and Hearing

In today's society people rely on their vision more than their hearing in most situations. Ironically, the sensory information we get from our ears is actually superior to that we receive from our eyes. The ears can sense vibrations that are much farther away (yang) and much more dispersed (yang) than visual information the eyes are able to receive. For instance, ears can hear the sounds from all angles whereas eyes can only see what is in front of them. From inside a room without windows, ears can still hear sounds from outdoors, while eyes cannot see what is beyond the walls. The ears are therefore more yang than the eyes in terms of sensory abilities.

Ears are also yang in terms of position since they are situated posterior to the eyes. Yin-yang theory states that back is yang and front is yin, so aforementioned consideration of eyes as the most yang was based on its highest position on the face. Just remember that yin and yang can change with differing perspective and this is another way to view positions.

In regard to bodily movement, however, we can see that vision and hearing have opposing natures. When trying to see better, people generally crane their necks to get a better look. This requires that the body becomes more active (yang). When attempting to hear sounds that are unfamiliar, people drop their heads and still their physical movements in order to pay closer attention (yin).

Conclusion

Like everything in nature, every part of our bodies has a yin and yang aspect. The brain, the most complex of all physical forms, is no exception and clearly comprises both yin and yang. Sense organs, which are really extensions of the brain, also have yin and yang aspects to them. Just as yin and yang complement and support each other to create and sustain all things, the two hemispheres of the brain and all the sense organs, whether yin or yang, must cooperate to help us better perceive, recognize and comprehend various things.

CHAPTER 5
Yin and Yang of Food and Diet

Possibly the most important thing we can do on a daily basis to balance our bodies' yin and yang energies is to maintain a healthy diet. Along with the air (yang) we breathe, food (yin) gives us the energy we need to maintain, repair and build our bodies, and to function in our daily lives. But what is a healthy and balanced diet?

A healthy diet starts with eating foods that are beneficial to our bodies; foods that balance our yin and yang energetic tendencies. Foods are categorized into yin and yang based on the source of the food, their taste, temperature, smell/odor, and the action they have on the body once they are digested. Once we determine the nature of a food, we can decide if it will support or harm our health and can make informed decisions about what is truly a healthy diet.

Looking at the Source

The source of a food is one way to determine its nature. The yin-yang continuum of food sources is illustrated in Fig. 5.1. Animals and animal products are yang in nature while foods from plant sources are more yin. Animals are considered yang due to their active, dynamic nature while plants are considered yin due to their passive nature. Foods from animal sources are also denser in nutrients (yang) than those derived from plant sources, which contain proportionally more fiber (yin) and water (yin). Looking at plant sources, grains contain less water (yin) and are therefore more yang than fruits and vegetables. Further, fruits are more yang than vegetables because they are sweeter.

YIN AND YANG OF FOOD AND DIET

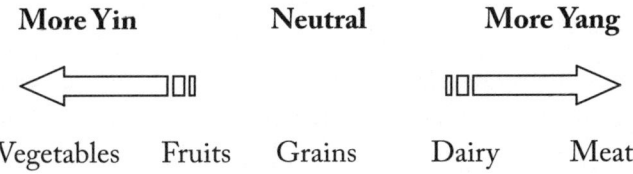

Figure 5.1 Yin-Yang Spectrum of the Basic Food Groups

The yin and yang of a various foods can also be determined by how the body processes the foods. Foods that are difficult or impossible to digest completely are molecularly sluggish, meaning that the foods' molecular components are slow and difficult to break down in the digestive process. Fats and oils are molecularly slow and therefore difficult to digest. Fiber cannot be digested at all because its molecular interactions are very slow. Following this line of reasoning we see that the more fat, oil or fiber a food contains, the more yin it is. In addition, foods the body is not able to fully process tend to have a slightly offensive and bitter (yin) taste hidden within. On the other hand, foods that digest easily, such as spices, have highly active molecules that help facilitate digestion. Therefore, foods that are pungent and/or sweet digest much more easily than those with a bitter or sour taste.

The source of the food and the digestion of the food have a reciprocal relationship stemming from the Inversion Principle. Foods that are more yang in nature are more yin in regards to their digestion and vice versa. For example, meat products (yang), which are primarily composed of fats and proteins, take longer (more yin) to digest than fruits and vegetables, which are primarily natural sugars, fiber and water. Because they take longer to break down, they require more water and energy for the process of digestion. In addition, the energy the body ultimately receives from this digestive process is slower to arrive (yin) and more prolonged (yin) once it begins. Yin natured foods, on the other hand, are broken down quickly, require little energy or water to digest and give the body quick energy. In addition, the sugars and water contained in yin natured foods actually aid in the digestion of yang natured foods. This is the reason people crave sweets, water, coffee or tea after eating a heavy meal.

Tastes and Cravings

Taste is crucial when determining which foods are beneficial and which are harmful. Tastes the body craves are often found in nutritional elements the body is lacking. For example, children and teenagers prefer hamburgers and processed sweets to carrots and cabbage because their bodies' rapid growth and development need large quantities of both rapid and sustained energy. Meat offers sustained nutrition (yin energy), while the sugar found in sweets feeds children's rapidly changing internal environment (yang energy).

The elderly crave meat and sugar less often. That is not to say that they don't enjoy steaks and ice cream, rather their internal systems have less of a need for the nutrients derived from these foods. In all, taste makes a person automatically select what is necessary for his or her body and differs from person to person and time to time.

Eastern medicine has been researching the effects of tastes for thousands of years with an understanding that taste plays an important role in determining the medicinal characteristics and physiological effects of foods and herbs. Just as western medicine analyzes the chemical composition of a drug to determine its function, eastern medicine analyzes tastes to determine the effects of foods or herbal medicines.

Taste is the result of the individual yin-yang variance that is the synthesis of the entire development and composition of a substance. Unlike western pharmaceuticals, foods and herbs are ingested in their entirety and eastern traditions consider them to be a medicine if they cause significant physiological changes in the body. Substances with a yin and yang balance similar to the human body that cause few bodily changes are considered foods.

One thing to note is that every element in food has an independent effect on the body. Because of the multitude of elements in foods, modern chemistry cannot analyze the total effect of any given food. Western science would need to break down the elements to a quantum physical level and study their relationships in order to determine the body's responses to various foods.

In eastern medicine, there are five basic tastes: pungent, sweet, sour, bitter and salty. They are classified into yin or yang depending on their effects on the body. For instance, foods that are spicy, sweet or salty will induce yang actions in the body while those that are sour or bitter will induce yin actions. A balanced meal includes all five flavors.

Pungent

Pungent foods are yang as they disperse energy and activate the yang functions and internal processes of the body. They stimulate the digestive system by increasing the production of saliva and digestive juices and by augmenting peristalsis, the muscular contractions that move food through the digestive tract. They also stimulate mental function and other physiological activities. For example, when we eat hot peppers or wasabi we feel stimulated and more awake and aware. We may start to sweat and our breathing may become more rapid. We also may feel like drinking a big glass of cold water–our system's way of attempting to neutralize the fire (yang) with water (yin).

Hot peppers (chili, jalapeño, habanero) are the epitome of pungent foods. Other examples include garlic, ginger, onion, cinnamon, black pepper, clove, nutmeg, turmeric, fennel and mustard. While pungency is the predominant flavor of these foods and thus their major categorization, all foods contain a number of flavors giving each food its own unique taste and medicinal action.

Sweet

Sweetness, in eastern medicine, is defined as anything sweeter than water and is the distinguishing factor between foods and non-foods or medicines. All foods, grains, meats, fruits and even bitter vegetables have some element of sweetness stemming from their carbohydrate component, which supplies energy and nourishment to the body.

In eastern medicine, the sweet taste is the most balanced flavor because it moderates and harmonizes extreme actions. It neutralizes toxins and stops pain and spasm. It is also easily assimilated and benefits digestion. Moreover, the sweet taste is the most nurturing and the best source of energy for the body. Examples include honey, licorice, maltose and sugar cane.

Honey is considered to be the sweetest food. It has many medicinal effects and is traditionally used to combat stomach spasms. The theory of yin and yang states that the body's energy is in a continuous cycle of contraction and expansion. Pain occurs when energy remains in a contracted (yin) state. Because the sweet taste is balanced, it is able to ameliorate any extreme of yin or yang. Drinking honey mixed with warm water during stomach spasms will dissipate pain like melting ice with hot water.

Honey's action on the body is different than processed sugar. During the refining process, sugar loses many of it natural qualities and nutrients. Honey is eaten in its unadulterated state and has far more medicinal effects and less harmful properties. Honey also contains enzymes that benefit the digestive system and its sugars are also more easily broken down and assimilated than those in processed sugar.

The overall yin and yang classification of sweet foods is determined by the level of sweetness. Although sweet is the most balanced taste, it is a fundamental source of energy and therefore incites yang actions in the body. Because of this, foods that are mildly sweet are mildly yang, and foods that are primarily sweet are more yang.

Sour

Sour is a yin and contracting flavor. It promotes the drawing of energy and fluids inward, slows the body's physiological activities and respiration, decreases blood pressure, and cools the body. Because of its accumulative effect, eastern medicine recommends the use of sour herbs for symptoms such as coughing or diarrhea, where energy or fluids are pathologically leaving the body.

After exercise, when the body's functions have sped up and its energy spent, sour drinks like lemonade taste great. The reason for this is that the sour taste slows down and constricts energy to help the body return to a balanced state. Children tend to like sour foods, such as pickles and Sour Patch Kids, because the yin energy of the food balances their yang nature. Sour taste actually aids in the materialization of substance for growth, regeneration and the productions of new cells. This is also the reason why elderly people do not like sour foods. They have less production of new cells and so have less need to gather the energy for materialization of substance.

Bitter

Bitter is also yin. It descends (yin) and cools (yin) the body's energy.

Diseases that are yang in nature are caused by excessive heat in the body and manifest with a high fever and rapid pulse. Western medicinal substances prescribed for these illnesses, such as quinine, corticosteroids and antibiotics, are extremely bitter and curb the excessive yang activity with their yin effects. Herbs that clear heat, reduce inflammation and detoxify are also bitter. However, since the whole plant is used and not just its component parts as in western pharmaceuticals, herbs have fewer and less severe side effects.

The properties of the bitter taste (cool and descending) can also promote bowel movements. That is why most purgatives, substances that strongly promote bowel movements, are bitter.

Extremely bitter substances elicit a strongly negative physical reaction in the body. This is a protective mechanism in place to protect us from ingesting foods that could strongly slow or stop our life energy (poisons or toxins).

Salty

Salt and water have opposing natures. Just as yin and yang are attracted to one another, water and salt are also drawn together. Old water (ocean and sea water) is salty because over time the water chemically attracted enough salt to change its composition. The body requires salt to retain water. Sodium and chloride, the elemental components of salt, are essential in maintaining the proper physiological functioning of the body.

Water is the substance most representative of yin. Salt, its opposite, is the quintessential yang substance. Water washes, erodes, absorbs and conceals all things into the ocean. Salt, the crystallization of sea water, is volatile. When salt is fried, it explodes. In the past, nitrate (which has a salty taste) and salt, were used as the main ingredients in explosives. Nitroglycerin (a nitrate) is used to dilate the blood vessels of the coronary artery during attacks of angina (pain in the chest resulting from a lack of blood to the heart). Sildenafil citrate (also known by the brand name Viagra) was first studied as an alternative to nitroglycerin in the treatment of angina. However, it was found to expand the blood vessels of male genitals and thus became the now-famous drug for impotence.

For these reasons, salt produces yang actions in the body such as increasing blood circulation and raising blood pressure. It can, however, also help dissolve hard masses or soften hard lumps and so is used medicinally for hard lymph nodes or hard stool. Because of its yang action, salt can also improve digestion of meats, grains and legumes.

Artificial Flavors

One exception to the principles that govern taste is found in pharmacologically active ingredients that have been extracted from plants and then artificially synthesized. The real tastes of artificial condiments, such as MSG and saccharin, are masked and their influences on the body differ completely from their tastes.

For instance, MSG is a sodium salt of glutamic acid which stimulates receptors in the taste buds specific for meat. Therefore, when MSG is ingested the body perceives that it has consumed a great deal of meat and reacts accordingly, releasing digestive enzymes and preparing for the influx of fuel. The activation of these physiological processes without the nutritional base to support the metabolic processes causes some of side effects we see in MSG-sensitive individuals, including chest pain, headaches, heartburn, facial pressure and excessive sweating.

Saccharin is an artificial sweetener that is 300 to 500 times sweeter than sugar. Saccharin stimulates taste buds that fool the body into perceiving that it has just ingested large quantities of sugar. As with MSG the body begins metabolic processes, including the release of insulin, in response to the perceived influx of calories with no nutritional base to support the processes.

Since saccharin's invention there has been a great deal of controversy about health risks associated with the artificial sweetener. For years the FDA tried unsuccessfully to ban saccharin. Many scientific studies show, however, that stimulation of the taste buds by artificial sweeteners induce increased insulin production. This can be very damaging to the body. In order to gain a better understanding of the potential harm, let's analyze this process using the principles of yin and yang. When a sugar (yang) enters the body there is a surge of energy while the sugar remains in the blood stream. Blood sugar levels must remain balanced, however, so the body produces insulin in order to transform and store the sugar. The transformation and storage of sugar are yin actions which slow the body's metabolism. When a person eats or drinks products containing saccharin, the body produces massive amounts of insulin in response.

The body, however, is lacking the nutritional base to support the influx of insulin. This can result in an insulin reaction (extremely low blood sugar) with signs and symptoms such as hunger, sweating and trembling. If the body's cells remain hungry over period of time, the structure of the cellular DNA may change in order to stay alive. This would result in a fundamental change in the cells and they may become cancerous.

Temperature/Nature/Energy

The "temperature" of a food is another important factor in determining the food's yin and yang characteristics. According to eastern medicine there are four basic temperatures of food: hot, warm, cool and cold. Hot or warm foods are yang and cold or cool foods are yin. Temperature indicates the reaction the food causes in the body rather than simply whether it comes from the freezer or the stove. For instance, eating watermelon and cucumbers or drinking beer will elicit a cold sensation, while eating chili peppers or cinnamon or drinking hard liquor will elicit a hot sensation.

Warm or hot (yang) foods speed up the metabolism, aid in digestion, improve blood circulation, promote sweating and increase energy levels and mental alertness. Cold or cool (yin) foods slow the metabolism, calm the nerves, reduce inflammation, fever and thirst, eliminate toxins and treat constipation and various skin conditions.

In general, foods from animal sources tend to be warmer and those from plant sources tend to be colder. Meats are generally warm and sea food is generally cool. Spices are hot (yang), while fruits and vegetables are generally cooler (yin).

Smell/Odor

Smells may be divided into yin and yang. Smells that people are attracted to are yang while unpleasant, offensive odors are yin. Generally, yang fragrances function to stimulate the nerves, while yin odors depress the nervous system's response. In other words, yang fragrances tend to support physiological activities, whereas yin odors suppress them. Thus, yang fragrances can facilitate digestive functioning, eliminate gas, and stop nausea. They can also promote sweating, disinfect, and even eliminate parasites. Yin odors, meanwhile, can calm the mind and emotions. They can also be used for fainting, coma and collapse.

Meat
Beef

Eastern traditions teach that the vibrational frequency of the sound that cows make is identical to the central frequency of the universe. Yoga practitioners chant the mantra "OM," which is similar to the "moo" of a cow, when seeking to achieve balance by resonating their bodies to the sound of the universe. A cow's vocal vibrational pattern is one reason beef is the most energetically balanced meat humans consume. The energetic composition of beef is very similar to that of the human body, though it is slightly more yin. Because of this similarity the human body savors the taste of beef. And because its yin-yang energy is well balanced, beef can be eaten by almost anyone without disrupting the body's natural energetic flow.

Cows have a gentle (yin) nature. But their yin is on the verge of transforming into yang. Their slow and droning movements are indicative of their yin nature, but they have horns which indicate that they are transforming into yang. The season that relates to the cow is the period halfway through the transformation from winter to spring when yang energy is beginning to awaken. Thus, the energy that was stored and dormant during the winter is beginning to activate and be consumed. The eastern zodiac cycle illustrates this by placing the cow in the north-northeast position. The significance of this is that, energetically, beef has the power to convert matter into energy.

Though it has not been scientifically proven, we can presume that obese people who want to eat meat should eat beef, since it has the power to transform substance into energy. If beef and no other food is eaten, the nutrients in beef will not be stored as fat, but will instead consume fat stores in the body, similar to the high protein - low carbohydrate diet. However, this is not a balanced or healthy way to lose weight and this example is simply meant to express the energetic properties of beef.

Pork

Pigs are fleshy and plump and are known for their gentle, relaxed and carefree nature. Pigs reside low to the ground, are generally dark in color and are fairly inactive. These are all yin traits, making pigs the most yin land animal (yang) so their energetic characteristic is yin within yang.

Because of the strong yin nature of pigs, pork is considered extremely nourishing. It readily adds weight to the body and stabilizes overactive metabolisms. Hyperactive children with low body weights would benefit from eating pork. It can help calm their active nature and allow them to concentrate and focus.

Pork's yin nature also nourishes the reproductive organs located in the body's yin region. Additionally, because pork is a meat and retains the yang function, the combination of its yin and yang actions give pork the ability to increase virility.

Poultry

Birds are more yang than other animals because they can fly, and thus the meat we derive from birds is more yang than any other meat source. Although chickens do not fly, they are birds and share many similar characteristics. Their inability to fly makes them more yin. However, chickens are extremely aggressive (yang) and their movements are rapid (yang). Therefore, chicken meat activates yang functions in the body.

Though wild ducks can fly, domesticated ducks cannot. Thus, domesticated ducks are more yin in nature. Ducks, in general, are considered yin birds (yin within yang). They live near water and have disproportionately large hips. The hip region is the area of the body with the least distribution of blood vessels and is therefore considered languid. Inactivity is yin in nature as is the lower half of the body. Therefore, the energy derived from duck meat tends to sink as its nutrients make their way to the reproductive organs. For this reason eating duck (yin) with white wine (yang) is a great aphrodisiac.

Seafood

Fish move akin to their nature. Although they can move quickly, they generally move slowly and use their bodies (trunk) more than their fins–analogous to the arms, wings and legs of land and air animals–for propulsion. As the trunk is more yin relative to arms and legs, fish are considered animals with well-developed yin. They also live in the cold and dark water (yin) of lakes and oceans.

Fresh water fish are more yin than salt water fish because they are not surrounded by salt (yang) and are less compressed by the forces of water due to the smaller bodies of water in which they live.

Although fish are yin, they are of a higher order than most other foods from the sea. They are vertebrates and are different from other, more primitive, marine animals such as squid and octopus, and shellfish like clams, shrimp and lobster. These more primitive organisms are more yin in nature than fish and contain a good deal of cholesterol, a yin, fat-like substance that provides the building material for cell membranes and can accumulate in our arterial walls. Because their nature is tilted to yin, they do not contain the yang energy required to move the blood and prevent the build up of cholesterol. Fish, on the other hand, are more balanced. Studies have shown that certain types of fish, such as salmon, herring, mackerel and sardines, contain high levels of omega-3 essential fatty acids that can actually lower the level of saturated fat and cholesterol in the body, which is a yang action of fish.

Sea cucumbers live in the ocean (yin) and are dark and creepy (yin). The sea cucumber is known as the "ginseng of the sea" in China and Korea. Like ginseng, the sea cucumber is a strong aphrodisiac. Its appearance also resembles the male genitals. The Doctrine of Signatures states that "like attracts like" or, in other words, things that are similar in appearance can give and take energy from each other. Thus sea cucumbers, with their resemblance to male genitals, are considered to have the ability to strengthen the male sexual organs.

Dairy Products
Milk

Milk is perhaps the most balanced food. It contains a well-rounded combination of energy and nutrients necessary for the growth and activity of children. Historically milk has been used for a wide range of disorders such as fatigue, underweight conditions, upset stomach, difficulty swallowing, diabetes and constipation. It is also used as a blood tonic.

Of the various types of milk, goat milk is the most yang, cow milk is the most yin, and human milk is the most balanced. Anything fed to an infant must be well balanced. Cows nurse for a much shorter period of time and grow much faster than humans. This is partially due to the immense growth potential that exists in cow's milk. Cow's milk is extremely yin for the human system. Because of this, many people have an allergy to the sugar (lactose) and the protein (casein) in milk and dairy products. Food allergies indicate the unbalanced nature of that particular food.

Soured milk products such as buttermilk, kefir, yogurt, cheese and cottage cheese are predigested by the bacterial action of the souring process and are, therefore, more easily digested (yang) in the body. Of these products, yogurt is the most yang and cheese is the most yin.

Eggs

Eggs and milk are both well balanced. However, milk is more yin while eggs are more yang. The yang of eggs applies only to the portion we eat, the white and yolk. Between these two portions, the white is more yang and the yolk is more yin. The egg white is in the outer portion and is less dense. It is also the part of the egg that, if fertilized, will develop into a chicken (a yang activity). The yolk is more central, denser and contains most of the cholesterol and nutrients we derive from eggs. It is also the nutritional source for the developing chicken. On the whole, eggs are more nutritious than milk. They are more balanced because they contain relatively equal amounts of both yin and yang, just like an atom, a zygote, the universe or the Tai Chi.

Nuts

Nuts are basically oily seeds surrounded by thick shells. Shells gather and consolidate energy (yin). The nuts inside are relatively more yang because they have the potential to sprout and disperse their energy. The thicker the shell, the stronger its yin action and the stronger the yang action of the nut inside. Nuts such as peanuts, walnuts, chestnuts, pine nuts, hazelnuts, pecans and pistachios invigorate blood circulation in the superficial regions of the body, accelerate the metabolism, and lower cholesterol.

All nuts have a thin brown lining between the nut and the shell that has an astringent (puckering) and bitter tastes. The astringent and bitter tastes and the brown (dark) color are yin. This thin lining also contains large amounts of tannin, a chemical that can stop bleeding and diarrhea. Its yin properties can benefit people who suffer from chronic coughing, diarrhea or bleeding. The lining can also be boiled and taken as a tea. Yang-natured people who are thin, restless, and have excellent circulation should eat nuts with this thin lining. This can prevent conditions of yin deficiency due to yang excess.

Grains

Determining the yin and yang nature of grains is a relatively arduous task today. Food preparation has advanced to the degree that the husks are completely removed from grains and their outer layers are sliced before they reach the store. This type of food processing makes the original tastes of grains difficult to determine. Only when the husks of the grains are intact can their tastes truly be discerned; but by looking at the fundamental nature of grains it is possible to determine their yin and yang characteristics.

Barley, wheat, buckwheat and oats are all relatively yin grains while rice, sweet rice and sorghum are relatively yang. Yin grains are more difficult to digest than yang grains and people with weak digestive systems tend to experience gas when they eat them. Oatmeal, for instance, is good for constipation because it does not digest completely and so serves as bulk.

Rice

Rice is a yang food that supplies the body with significant amounts of yang energy. There are, however, many varieties of rice that supplement the body's energy differently. Rice is processed by trimming the outer layers of the husk to varying degrees. As the layers are removed, the rice becomes whiter, more easily digestible and more yang in nature. Wild rice retains its husk and is therefore more difficult to digest. Because of this, the energy we derive from eating wild rice is more balanced in yin (husk) and yang (inner rice). Brown rice maintains a portion of its husk, while all forms of white rice are the most thoroughly processed.

Long-grain rice is more easily digestible than short-grain or glutinous rice. Although they are both white, they are shaped differently. Yin-yang theory maintains that round objects are more yin as they condense or gather energy, while long objects are yang as their energy extends to the outside. According to these principles long grain rice is considered more yang than short-grain or glutinous rice.

Like seeds, whole grains have a well-balanced distribution of yin and yang. Seeds and grains lose their ability to support and initiate life if there is too great a discrepancy in yin and yang. If we eliminate the outside of the food (yin) and only eat the inside portion (yang), the nature of that food becomes too tilted in one direction, causing harm to our bodies. Therefore, eating too much white or polished rice or white flour without other foods to balance their side effects can lead to problems, as discussed later in the food and disease section.

Wheat

Wheat grows well in cooler climates such as Northern Europe. Because of this, it is more yin in nature than rice, which grows well in warmer climates such as Southeast Asia. Wheat is also slightly more bitter (yin) than rice. Because of its yin characteristics, people who eat wheat as a staple of their diets tend to gain weight.

The yin nature of wheat can treat various illnesses that arise from excessive yang. For example, the mind is yang compared to the body. Therefore, the mind likes to remain calm (yin). People who are constitutionally tilted toward yang or those who are under a great deal of stress have more yang energy in their bodies, and it is more difficult for them to remain calm. These people can easily develop heart palpitations, insomnia and irritability. Eating wheat and wheat products can help alleviate these symptoms. The outer layer of wheat is more yin than the inner layer, so for people who suffer from these conditions it would be more beneficial to eat whole wheat.

Premenstrual Syndrome (PMS) among women develops as a result of dysfunction in the reproductive system, a yin region of the body. Eating wheat can help strengthen and invigorate the system and alleviate the symptoms of PMS. However, wheat is a food and not a medicine, so its yin action is mild. It must be ingested for a long time in order to be effective.

Oats

Compared to rice, oats are not as sweet and contain a bitter flavor (yin). They are a rough grain and have many tasteless fibers. These fibers are considered to be yin in nature as their structure is tightly knit, making them difficult to digest. Because oats are not entirely digested, they are effective for relieving constipation. Fibers are located on the outside, like a shell or peel, which are yin because they protect and compress the inside contents. Oats' yin nature is effective against diabetes or heart disease caused by the over consumption of refined sugar (yang) or refined meat (yang). Oats help mend the imbalance of the modern diet that is oversupplied with yang energy.

Barley

Barley is yin in nature. It is cool and the most difficult grain to digest. Eating barley will make a person's stomach stay full for a longer period of time. It also prevents constipation because it contains a lot of fiber. These characteristics clearly point to its yin nature.

Corn

Corn is a more primitive (yin) plant than the other grains. It has a larger body (yin), more rounded leaves (yin), and corn silk (yin) growing through the top of the ear. Because of these features corn more closely resembles yin-natured vegetables than do the other grains and is thought to be on the border between grains and vegetables. Corn is a good side dish to meat because it contains yin characteristics similar to vegetables and will establish harmony with meat's yang qualities.

Corn dried in the sunlight becomes very hard (yin) due to its strong consolidating energy. When heat (yang) is applied, it explodes to become popcorn. Corn's ability to secure its dual nature stems from its internal balance. This balance is maintained by the strong yin energy derived from the outer aspect of the corn kernel and the strong yang energy that resides inside within its clearly visible germ. This germ is what explodes outward and sprouts through the peel of corn and so is a quintessentially yang substance.

In eastern medicine the Kidneys are considered to be yin in nature but they also contain the body's innate yin and yang energetic stores. Corn has a similar construct not only energetically but also in its shape, and therefore it acts on the Kidneys. The strong yin nature of corn's outer peel has a diuretic effect on the body. The more yin corn silk is an even stronger diuretic. Because of these actions, corn can be used to treat such diseases as urinary difficulty or hypertension due to excessive yang, and kidney stones. The minerals (yin) derived from corn, such as iron, potassium and magnesium, can be acquired in greater amounts by eating young corn because it has less starch (yang).

Fruits

Fruits are primarily sweet (yang) with varying degrees of tartness (yin). Their sweetness provides energy to the body and their sour flavor activates a gathering energy in the body. Their high water content (yin) also serves to supply the body with water.

Lemons

Lemons are much more sour than sweet. They elicit a strong contracting action in the body. Excess consumption of lemons may damage our natural balance. This is why we cannot tolerate more than a few drops of lemon juice at a time.

Lemons are also extremely fragrant. Powerful scents indicate vigorous molecular activity. The smell of fish is yin because it suppresses digestive functioning. A few drops of lemon juice on fish will neutralize the yin odor and improve the body's ability to digest the fish. Another positive effect of lemon's strong fragrant smell is that it has antiseptic and anti-microbial action and so is used for dysentery and parasite infestations.

The gathering property of the sour taste of lemons combines well with the dispersing action of alcohol–vodka in particular. Palpitations and nausea that come from excessive intoxication can be quieted with lemon juice. It has a calming, sobering effect and can pacify the stomach.

Limes

Limes have a similar taste and similar functions to lemons. They are cooling and clear summer heat, promote bodily fluids to relieve thirst, can regulate the stomach and prevent miscarriages. Both lemons and limes are considered to be highly beneficial to pregnant women.

When a woman becomes pregnant, her blood volume increases by 20 to 30 percent. This results in an increased cardiac output and more pressure on the vessel walls. When yang becomes extreme, energy moves outward, leaving the inside empty and malnourished. As a result, the stomach becomes weak. This is why women often cannot eat early in their pregnancy. In the first term of pregnancy they experience nausea and vomiting because of the sudden change in their blood volume. These symptoms gradually disappear as their bodies adapt.

Nausea and vomiting tend to be worse in the morning when the body's yang energy is activated and blood volume and circulation increase. That is why it is called "morning sickness." For the same reason, people's pulses are stronger when they first wake up than later in the day when yang energy is weaker. Carbonated water mixed with lime is excellent for calming the symptoms of morning sickness. It is good for pregnant women to drink as much of this concoction as possible, at least three times a day for several days until the symptoms subside. They should also smell lemons as often as they can.

Similar to lemons, limes are used in alcoholic beverages, such as gin and tonic, and are served with drinks such as tequila and Mexican beer.

* A word of caution: Due to their high acid content, those who suffer from excess stomach acid or ulcers need to be very careful with both lemons and limes.

Oranges

Oranges have similar actions to lemons. They are, however, sweeter and less sour, and thus more yang. Orange peels added to beef dishes create a very desirable taste because the peels supplement the shortage of yang digestive energy in beef. In eastern medicine, dried orange peels are combined with other herbs to treat digestive problems as well as illnesses resulting from the excessive intake of alcohol.

Apples

Apples grow in cool climates. They have a sour taste and a cool temperature, so they belong to the category of yin fruits. Due to their yin nature, apples can help the body produce fluids, moisten dryness and clear heat in the lungs. Thus they can treat thirst, cough and dry mouth, and neutralize toxic effects from cigarettes.

Apples also have a sweet taste that affects the digestive system. They can be useful in treating indigestion, loss of appetite and diarrhea. Regardless of their medicinal value, apples are typically difficult to digest due to their yin nature. Cooking them reduces their yin nature, sweetens their taste, and makes them easier to digest. This is why there are many cooked or baked apple products, like applesauce and apple pie. Among the varieties of apples, Fuji apples are sweeter and less sour than other types of apples and are the most easily digested. In general, people with weak digestive systems should not eat many apples or should eat them cooked or at least remove the peel.

Pears

Pears contain a lot of water and fiber. The more fiber a fruit contains the stronger its yin nature. Asian pears have more water and larger particles of fiber within their pulp than other pears; thus they are more yin. Pears have the ability to strengthen the respiratory system and stop chronic coughing. The lungs and respiratory system are considered yin within yang. They are located above the diaphragm (yang) but have the yin function of absorbing oxygen. People who suffer from a chronic cough have a lack of yin gathering energy and damaged yang energy. An Eastern remedy for this type of illness is well-cooked pears with honey (yang). Cooked pears are also good for residual coughing after the common cold or flu.

Peaches

Peaches have a sharp tip and a lot of hair or "fuzz." These features indicate that peaches have a strong dispersing or yang energy than other fruits. When yin people suffer from poor digestion, they should eat peaches. If the sour taste is unappealing, they can eat canned peaches that have been fully ripened and soaked in sweeteners. Canned peaches are excellent for convalescent patients to recover their energy. Eastern medicine uses peach seeds for eliminating stagnant blood because they help promote blood circulation. In the East peaches are said to chase spirits away. At ancestral memorial services they are not placed on the table alongside other foods. The reason is that the yang nature of peaches is believed to expel the yin-natured spirits who are being honored.

Grapes

Grapes grow on vines. Vines characteristically encircle their fruit and have thorns that hook them together. They grow inward and have a pulling nature so they coil onto things near them and pull those things inward. Grape vines are fundamentally plants with stems, leaves and fruit that are curled tightly together. Grapes are cold in nature and the leaves of grape vines are sour. All of these traits give grapes a very yin nature. The darker the grape, the more yin it is. Grapes are excellent for people with fiery characters caused by an overabundance of dispersing (yang) energy and a lack of gathering (yin) energy who also have weakness in their knees and low backs. The knees and low back are in yin regions of the body and are vulnerable to weakness in people who lack yin. The yin/gathering nature of grapes can assist these people in balancing their yin and yang energies.

Cherries and Kiwis

Cherries and kiwis are two other examples of fruits that gather energy. Yang natured people (such as those described above) should eat cherries, kiwis and grapes on a regular basis to prevent and/or treat yang natured diseases.

Muskmelons

Muskmelons also grow on vines. They have a bitter taste near their stems but do not have strong gathering action as they contain almost no sour taste. Nevertheless they do have yin nourishing actions due to their cool nature and the abundance of moisture they contain. Because of their strong yin nature, if a yin natured person eats too much muskmelon they would most likely get a stomach ache and diarrhea.

Watermelon

Though watermelon has a cold temperature (yin) which can cool the body, it also has a strong dispersing action (yang) because it is encased in a thick peel. Like thick-shelled nuts, the thick-peeled watermelon disperses energy. It is red, the color of fire, and crisp. This crispness indicates that it has vigorous molecular activity, a yang trait. Because of this, watermelon is beneficial to the heart and assists it by improving blood circulation. This moves more blood through the kidneys and increases urine output. Therefore, watermelons are great for obese people who suffer from a slow metabolism and have heart disease, high blood pressure or diabetes.

Vegetables

Vegetables in general are more yin than meat or fruits. Due to their yin nature, they have a harmonious effect when combined with various meat and fish dishes. Their harmonizing effects include improving digestion, reducing odor and detoxifying.

Radishes

Radishes are edible roots that have a sweet and pungent taste. Roots gather energy from the ground and raise it upward (yang). The pungent taste (yang) of radishes stimulates the digestive functions of the stomach. People with weak digestive systems can benefit tremendously from eating radishes.

Wasabi and horseradish are stronger, more yang forms of radish since they are extremely pungent (yang). Either wasabi alone or a combination of horseradish and mustard made into a paste complements raw fish. Fish are yin in nature and sashimi (raw, uncooked fish) is very yin. Sashimi by itself can injure the body because of its strong yin nature. The pungent, yang taste of wasabi is eaten to counter the strong yin nature of raw fish.

Cucumber

In general, foods that grow on vines typically have a strong yin nature because of the gathering action of the vine. Vines depend on other structures to support them. They cannot stand on their own, nor do they grow straight upwards. These are all yin qualities. Cucumbers grow on vines but they do not have a strong gathering action because they are not very sour. Their yin action is derived from their bitter taste, their cooling and descending nature, and their abundance of moisture. Cucumbers can help stop thirst and promote urination. They also detoxify and cool the blood. When applied externally, cucumbers can cool inflammation and treat burns.

Carrots

Carrots are orange in color and grow in the shape of an upside down triangle. Both of these attributes symbolize yang. Orange is very similar to red, which in the Tai Chi symbolizes yang. The upside down triangle is symbolic of the upward spreading nature of fire. In addition, the leaves of the carrot are narrow and spread out in several directions. This is yang in relation to the wide leaves of other plants.

In humans, the eyes correspond to the element Fire because they are the brightest part of the body. Carrots can improve the eyes' functioning. Night blindness is the first symptom of eye weakness, and carrots are especially beneficial for this ailment. The reason is that the yang of carrots can overcome the yin of the night.

According to the Doctrine of Signatures, like treats like. In the body, the Liver has the shape of an upside down triangle and is a yang organ. Carrots, which are similarly shaped, can strengthen the Liver. Carrots also contain a lot of fibers that correspond to the skin, tendons and fascia of the human body. Thus, in eastern medicine they are used to treat skin disorders and relieve fatigue of the motor system.

Potatoes

Potatoes are an extremely yin vegetable. They have wide, soft leaves (yin) and an unpleasant bitter taste (yin). Potatoes with dark blue or purple skins (yin colors) and the eyes of germinated potatoes contain a toxin called solanine (a yin toxin). Solanine can cause poisoning with symptoms including vomiting, abdominal pain, diarrhea, headaches, and even mental disorders. The tongue senses the potato's bitter taste to prevent the ingestion of toxins that will harm the body. Because of their yin nature, the taste of potatoes improves when they are combined with yang foods. Baking potatoes adds some yang. However, much more yang is added when potatoes are made into French fries by frying (yang) them in oil and then adding salt (also yang). As potatoes are yin in nature, a person with a yang constitution who suffers from excess secretion of stomach acid and intestinal ulcers can be treated by drinking potato juice every morning. Potatoes can also be used to heal inflammatory conditions such as burns.

Garlic

Garlic is extremely yang in nature. It has a strong smell and a mixture of pungent and sweet tastes. Its characteristics enable it to have a strong effect on the digestive system. It is also known to have an antiseptic and anti-cancer effect. Cancer cells are generally harder than the surrounding cells and are thought to be yin. Through its strong yang action, garlic can kill bacteria and intestinal worms and help prevent certain types of cancer. Garlic can improve the body's metabolism and blood circulation, and it warms the body. Therefore, garlic may be helpful for yin-natured people who have a tendency to be cold (body, hands and feet), have poor circulation, poor digestion and low energy.

An interesting side note: The nature of Dracula and all other vampires is extremely yin. They are soulless creatures that only thrive at night and live in dark, damp places. Garlic is an extreme yang substance that can neutralize strong yin substances. That is why folk tales tell of vampires threatened by garlic.

Ginger

Ginger, like garlic, is yang in nature. It is warm with a very pungent and mildly sweet taste. Its warmth is highly beneficial for the digestive system. It is one of the best foods to stop vomiting. It is similar to garlic in that it can kill bacteria and has anti-cancer properties. It reduces the smell of fish (yin) and can detoxify seafood poisoning (yin). It can induce mild sweating and is used to eliminate the common cold (yin). Like garlic, ginger is best for those who are yin in nature.

Meat that is slightly spoiled will have an offensive smell that suppresses digestive functioning. Eating it can damage the body. Garlic and ginger have an antibacterial effect and, used in large amounts, can combat bacteria that has begun to grow in the meat. Bacteria and germs generally like to grow in dark damp places, indicating their propensity towards yin. When you use a substance that is yang in nature to neutralize the effect, the bacteria can no longer flourish.

Lettuce

Lettuce has wide leaves, contains mostly water, and has a slightly bitter taste and cool temperature—all yin characteristics. Vegetables as a whole are more yin than other foods and lettuce is even more yin. The extreme yin of lettuce can serve as a tranquilizer to treat problems that are due to an excess of yang, such as insomnia, anxiety and restlessness. Most of the lettuce found in America has been modified to eliminate the bitter taste and has thus lost some of its yin functions. Yin-natured foods can strengthen the function of the kidneys, large intestine, and women's reproductive system, which all belong to yin. They are, therefore, effective for treating edema, urinary difficulty, constipation, yeast infection and hemorrhoids.

Tomatoes

Tomatoes are the reddest (yang) and most salty (yang) vegetable. They can help facilitate digestion and stimulate the appetite. Because of these functions, tomatoes are cooked and made into ketchup. Meats are the most difficult food to digest. Thus, putting ketchup on meat helps digestion. Higher-quality meats such as steak are more yang, and processed meats such as hamburger are more yin because they contain tendons, ligaments and fat. Therefore, the yang in ketchup helps with the digestion of hamburgers. Ketchup also helps balance the yin of potatoes and thus goes well with French fries.

Alcoholic Beverages

All alcoholic beverages are yang. The more alcohol contained in the beverage (the higher the proof) the more yang it is. Alcohol is molecularly active. This means that the chemical composition of alcohol readily combines with water. In the body, it speeds up blood circulation because of its rapid molecular activity. Western medicine, however, considers alcohol a depressant. After the initial stimulation, alcohol depresses the central nervous system because when yang reaches its extreme, it converts into yin.

Alcoholic beverages have a pungent taste that stimulates the secretion of digestive juices and increases peristalsis. When it is taken with food, especially meat, it behaves like a spice and aids in digestion. While the effects of other yang-type foods may be relatively slow, the effects of alcohol appear quickly. Alcohol is actually absorbed through the stomach lining into the blood stream. Drinking distilled spirits with nothing in the stomach to buffer them can disintegrate the stomach lining. Therefore, they are better taken with foods like cheese or meat than on an empty stomach. Drinking white liquor on an empty stomach is the quickest way to get an ulcer. But nothing beats it as an aid in digesting meat.

Beer

Beer is the most Yin alcoholic beverage. One reason is that it is derived from barley malt–a product of barley. As previously stated, barley is a very yin grain. It grows in cooler weather and sprouts during winter–the most yin season. Beer also contains hops which are fermented with barley to give beer its bitter flavor. Hops are bitter (yin) and have a sedating effect (yin).

Because beer contains alcohol it has a brief stimulating effect–yang–followed by the depressant effect derived from the yin actions of hops and barley. Some people use beer as a substitute for sleeping pills as it relaxes the body and mind.

Wine

Grapes are sour and astringent. These properties belong to yin and function to gather and consolidate energy. Alcohol accelerates energy transformation and temporarily strengthens the body. This is the reason that people tend to lose their inhibitions when they are drunk. Wine is more yang than beer, but more yin than spirits (distilled liquor). Darker colors are more yin and brighter colors are more yang. Because of their hues, white wine is more yang than blushed wine, which is in turn more yang than red wine. Although red is the color of fire, red wine has a descending, gathering nature and a calming effect as it is made from dark grapes. White wine and, to a lesser extent, blush wine are lighter and have an ascending action. They go right to the head, making a person feel giddy. The yang nature of white wine complements the yin nature of fish, and the yin nature of red wine balances the yang energies of beef.

Yin foods such as pork, oysters, sea cucumbers, duck, tortoise and eel supply nutrients to the reproductive organs. These nutrients, however, take a while to reach their destination. Drinking white wine, such as the famous wine of China called Maotai (120 proof), together with any of these yin foods, will hasten the activation of the body's sexual energies, like throwing gasoline on a fire. Many of these foods are cooked with spices to enhance their aphrodisiac qualities.

Vodka

Vodka is strongly yang. Its energy rises straight to the head. There is no better liquor for people that live in cold regions and for those whose physiological activities easily stagnate. Because it is extremely yang the body tends to reject the taste. Its nature can be sedated by mixing it with lemon or lime. A person with too much yang energy will be at greater risk for damaging their system if they consume excess amounts of any alcohol, especially vodka.

Whiskey

Whiskey is darker than vodka because it is made in oak barrels that have been smoked. Its color indicates that it is more yin than vodka. The longer whiskey is kept in a dark cellar (yin) the more balanced its yin and yang will be and the better it will taste. Whiskey is distilled from fermented grain mash (yin) and has many yin characteristics. Its energy can descend to the genital region (a yin region) and stimulate sexual desire by the yang action of the alcohol. Thus, a small amount of whiskey may be used as an aphrodisiac.

Sodas/Soft Drinks

Sodas supply the body with water (yin) and sugar (yang). This yin-yang balance makes them taste very good so that almost everyone enjoys drinking them. Because they provide water and quick energy, we tend to crave sodas more after exercise when we have sweated and are fatigued. With intense exercise our energy becomes concentrated in the external regions of our bodies, namely our arms and legs, which are yang. At the same time, the function of our digestive system (yin) declines. Sodas' carbonation gives them a sharp, biting taste, which is yang and so stimulates digestion. It is also the reason sodas taste better than simple sugar water.

Cola

Cola is made by adding kola bean extracts to carbonated water. Kola bean is a type of cacao bean that belongs to the nut family. As previously mentioned, nuts have a strong dispersing energy (yang) because they are surrounded by a hard shell (yin). This function is enhanced in the kola bean due to the presence of caffeine, one of its main ingredients. This yang function is normally antagonized by the yin function of the kola bean's oil (yin). However, the oil is removed during the processing of kola and cacao beans when producing cola or chocolate. Therefore, the dispersing energy is enhanced.

Further contributing to cola's yang action are its carbonation, and phosphoric and/or citric acid. Other ingredients commonly added to cola such as cinnamon, vanilla and nutmeg also have strong yang natures. Moreover, cola contains oils that have a strong aromatic fragrance (yang) such as orange, lime, or lemon fruit peel. Thus, all in all, these ingredients give cola a very potent yang action.

Cola's strong yang action can dissolve or transform the body's fats (yin) into energy. This fat dissolving function is what makes the cola taste good after eating greasy meat. But drinking too much cola on empty stomach can literally melt the inner lining of the stomach or duodenum causing ulcers. In addition to melting fat, cola's strong yang action can actually damage bone (yin) structure. This can be easily demonstrated by holding cola in your mouth for a while and then grinding the upper and lower teeth together. The teeth's surfaces will feel rough and worn.

Although cola is yang in nature it possesses yin qualities that serve to balance it out. Cola is dark due to its caramel coloring and has a slightly sour and astringent taste. These yin characteristics constrain the yang action of cola and prevent it from being toxic to our bodies. Without them, cola would not be fit for human consumption.

Dr Pepper

Although Dr Pepper appears similar in color to colas, it has a reddish hue indicating its yang nature. It also has a very pungent and spicy taste and can therefore facilitate digestive functioning. Dr Pepper is the best choice for people with weak digestive systems who generally dislike adding ice to soda.

Ginger Ale, Seven Up, Sprite

Ginger Ale, Seven Up and Sprite all have a lemon-lime flavor. As previously mentioned both lemons and limes calm the digestive system to treat symptoms such as nausea and vomiting. Theoretically, these three sodas can settle the stomach. Of the three, however, ginger ale is the most effective because it contains ginger–a famous digestive tonic with a yang nature. Ginger ale has traditionally been used for motion sickness and stomach upset. It has also been used to stop coughs and soothe sore throats. All of these actions of ginger ale coincide with use of ginger in traditional eastern medicine, where it is commonly used as a cold remedy. It is the most yang of the three lemon-lime sodas because it contains ginger.

Root Beer

Traditionally brewed root beer is completely different from other soft drinks. It is a type of tonic or elixir made by fermenting herbs such as juniper berry, sassafra root, and ginger with yeast. Not only is root beer a drink that replenishes consumed energy but it is also a medicine that can strengthen the stomach and lungs. Since root beer has a high concentration of nutrients, it has a slightly nauseating taste, which can somewhat burden the digestion. Thus the fragrance of wintergreen has been added to help facilitate digestion.

Juniper berry is yin in nature since it is a fruit which gathers energy into matter. Fragrant herbs such as sassafras, ginger and wintergreen are yang as they have dynamic molecular activity. Root beer ultimately can strengthen various functions of the body but it can not instantly quench thirst or stimulate digestion like other soft drinks.

From the perspective of digestive system, root beer is the most yin, cola is second, clear sodas are next and Dr Pepper is the most yang. Unfortunately, constant consumption of cold soft drinks will ultimately weaken the digestive system. Their cold temperature weakens the yang energy which then weakens the digestive fire. In addition, carbonated water can overwork the digestive system causing gas, bloating, abdominal pain and diarrhea, which is exacerbated by the caffeine contained in some soft drinks.

Diet and Disease

According to eastern medicine, disease results when there is an imbalance of yin and yang in the body. To restore health a proper diagnosis of the yin and yang imbalance must first be made, after which specific dietary and lifestyle guidelines are recommended to restore balance.

Ideally, foods and herbs should be taken in their entirety because the whole food or plant is more balanced than any of its component parts. For example, the interior of a kernel of rice, a seed, or a nut is considered to be yang because it contains stored energy that is ready to penetrate outward and sprout. The exterior is yin because it holds energy inside. If individual components of foods are isolated and consumed, they may create disturbances in the system and disease may develop. Consuming the whole foods and herbs will provide a natural nutritional and energetic balance. Unfortunately, modern society processes and refines foods to such a degree that their original natures are all but lost.

Human activity must also be balanced in yin and yang. In order to acquire energy (yin action), energy must be used up and consumed (yang action). Today, there is little need for most people to exert any energy when obtaining food from a store or restaurant. Therefore, calories are more easily accumulated than burned up.

Diabetes and hypertension are two examples of diseases common to yin natured people who overeat and accumulate (yin) a surplus of nutrients without burning them up (yang). Diabetes results from the body's inability to make or process insulin. There are two types of diabetes: one is thought to be genetic (Type I insulin-dependent diabetes) and the other is closely linked to diet and exercise (Type II). Type II diabetes is more than four times as common as Type I diabetes. When blood sugar levels increase, insulin is released into the blood stream. The presence of insulin allows sugar to move from the blood into the cells of the body. Insulin is therefore seen as a yin hormone because of its gathering nature. Exercise activates the cells of the body and burns up carbohydrates, which are complex sugars. Thus, after exercise it is easier for insulin to do its job of transporting the remaining glucose into the body's cells.

Diabetes was rare during the days of hunting and gathering because obtaining food required physical exertion. In order to obtain even a small piece of meat people had to hunt, sometimes for days. Hunting brings about a heightened state of awareness and improves the functioning of the body's systems. Additionally, people used to work long hours in fields to harvest grain. After harvesting grains the hulls had to be removed and the grain manually pounded with a mortar and pestle. Since people worked off all of the calories that they ate, insulin was secreted in proper amounts. So in order to prevent diabetes, it is important to avoid highly refined foods (yang) and to get enough exercise.

High blood pressure is another disease common to yin people because they have a tendency to gather energy and transform this energy into substance, such as cholesterol and arterial plaque. High blood pressure is a direct result of clogged blood vessels. These clogged vessels cause a drop in the blood supply to tissue cells. The cells signal the brain that they are not receiving the nutrients they need and, in response, the brain commands the heart to beat faster in order to increase blood supply to the cells. The heart responds, but the narrowed blood vessels impede circulation and cause pressure to build up (high blood pressure). If this cycle continues the coronary artery, which supplies blood to the heart, will also accumulate cholesterol. When the heart tries to pump blood under these conditions it easily becomes fatigued, eventually leading to angina or heart failure.

Yin-natured people tend to conserve and store fat and cholesterol instead of dissolving it and transforming it into energy. Their blood vessels become congested, putting undue pressure on blood vessel walls. Their metabolic actions also tend to be slower, which contributes to the build up.

Nuts and Cholesterol

Nuts sprout by penetrating through thick shells. Their penetrating force (yang) is extremely strong. This force can pierce the cholesterol-clogged (yin) blood vessels. The accumulated fats and cholesterol (yin) in the blood transform into energy (yang) and cholesterol levels drop. The cholesterol sticking to blood vessel walls (particularly the coronary artery) dislodge and dissolve. As the coronary artery opens up, angina disappears and heart attacks are prevented. Vegetable oils found in nuts are unsaturated fatty acids and can transform the saturated fatty acids that attach to arterial walls.

Several studies have documented the cholesterol-lowering effects of walnuts. One study presented at the Third International Congress on Vegetarian Nutrition in 1997 at Loma Linda Medical School in California was titled "Nut Consumption, Cardiovascular Disease Prevention and Longevity" by Joan Sabate, (professor and Chair of Nutrition at Loma Linda University, School of Public Health.)

In this study, which was conducted with approximately 31,000 California Adventists, researchers found that there was a significant reduction in the risk of myocardial infarction (heart attack) and death from ischemic heart disease (insufficient blood supply to heart) with increased nut consumption.

Natural Substances versus Pharmaceutical Drugs

Ingesting natural substances (foods and herbs) has a much less volatile effect on the body than chemically altered substances. Western pharmaceutical drugs are isolated components, many of which are artificially synthesized substances normally found in whole plants that significantly alter the state of yin and yang in the body. Pharmaceutical drugs do not, however, nourish a deficiency of the body, which would give the body a chance to regulate itself. In addition, the isolated components in these drugs are unrestrained by other elements that are naturally found in plants and thus create a deficiency themselves due to their imbalanced yin-yang nature. The strong effects of western drugs create a turbid internal environment. The body responds to this disruption of yin and yang by exhibiting unpleasant physical symptoms known as side effects.

Feed Your Needs

Human beings are tilted. Although they are the most centered of all organisms on Earth, each person possesses certain characteristics that are more yin or more yang. The combination of these characteristics defines the person. Physiological processes are generally weaker in people with a lot of yin. This most strongly affects their digestive system. Thus, they tend to have a more difficult time digesting meat and their digestive systems are better suited to break down foods from plant sources than animal products. Yin-natured people also tend to have a preference for sweet and pungent foods, which speed up the metabolism. As previously mentioned, sweet foods are yang because they are the energy source needed for physiological activity. Pungent foods are yang because they speed up the secretion of digestive juices and promote blood circulation.

Yang-natured people have a faster metabolism and a strong digestive system. They generally have less difficulty digesting meat. These people also have preferences for bitter and sour foods that slow down the metabolism. As previously mentioned, bitter foods are yin because they tend to be cooler and have a descending action, while sour foods gather energy inward and slow down blood circulation.

Groups can also be categorized according to yin and yang. These are generalizations and there is always yin within yang and yang within yin. Vegetarians are thought to be more yin than meat eaters because of the nature of the foods they eat. Fruits, vegetables and grains are more yin than meat products. Consuming these foods can make people more yin and put less stress on their stomach functions.

Easterners are considered more yin compared to Westerners. In general, eastern people eat more vegetarian dishes while western people eat more meat. Meat dishes are not standard fare in the eastern diet; rather they are reserved for special occasions. Eastern meat dishes are also prepared to facilitate their digestion with marinade and spices, while western meats are marinated less often.

Carbohydrates, proteins and fats can also be classified into yin and yang. Fats are the most yin and carbohydrates are the most yang. Calories represent the amount of energy that can be derived from a certain food. Fats have nine kilocalories, or kcal (a unit of heat), in every gram. This implies that fats contain a higher concentration of energy. Things that are more concentrated are molecularly slower and thus more yin. Proteins have four kcal per gram and are more yang than fats, but more yin than carbohydrates. Although carbohydrates contain a similar number of calories (3.9 kcal per gram), they are a more easily accessible form of energy and are thus more yang.

When there is a serious threat to your health due to an insufficient supply of essential nutrients, you will crave certain foods, whether or not they are present in your environment. When there is less of a need, cravings will only develop when you see or smell food that can properly serve the deficiencies of your system. Therefore, it is beneficial to visit a buffet restaurant that stocks a wide variety of foods whenever possible. If you can get to an exotic buffet that stocks foods you would not ordinarily see, so much the better. At the buffet, you should see and smell the foods and try to select the ones that appeal to you. If something tastes good to you, then your body is probably lacking in the elements it contains. Eat each food until it does not taste good anymore. When you lose your craving or taste for a food, it implies that your body has ingested a sufficient amount of the essential elements found in that food. Eating more would be harmful for you. You should go through the line more than once, again seeing and smelling the food to find the ones that appeal to you. This way you can ensure that your body gets its fill of all the nutrients it requires.

Cooking According to Yin and Yang

The yin-yang spectrum for cooking preparation is as follows: The more fire that comes into contact with a food, the more yang the cooking method. Broiling is the most yang, then dry roasting, then grilling (unless the chef torches the food). Frying is the next yang method, then baking, sautéing, and finally, steaming. Foods that are eaten raw (fresh-most yin, or dried-less yin) are obviously the most yin or coolest in temperature, as they do not come into contact with heat at all.

Meats eaten without salt or spices are more difficult to digest. The body borrows the yang action of salt or spices in order to thoroughly digest meat. They are molecularly dynamic and very fragrant. They facilitate digestion by increasing the secretion of digestive juices and facilitating peristalsis.

In order for flesh to function as part of a living animal, salt is absolutely essential. Meat that is still a part of a living animal receives a supply of salt through blood vessels. When carnivores kill their prey, a good supply of blood (and salt) is still pulsing through the muscle of the animal. Humans, however, eat processed foods in which the blood has been drained and the salt supply radically reduced.

Aside from salt and spices, cooking plays a big role in the process of digestion. A steak that is rare is more yin to digest than one that is well done. Therefore, the more cooked a piece of meat is, the easier it is to digest. This is why yin people, who tend to have weaker digestive functioning, generally prefer meat that is marinated, seasoned and more cooked than do yang individuals.

Many Chinese dishes are cooked over a strong fire using a wok. The shape of the wok enhances the strength of the fire. Flames actually ignite inside the wok and act as a slight disinfectant, killing the yin bacteria. The aroma produced by this method of cooking serves a similar function to adding spices to food as it stimulates the digestive system. Other cultures ignite alcohol over food for the same reason. This method of cooking is effective if done correctly. If not, food that is undercooked will taste horrible, while burned food will taste bitter.

Chinese meat dishes are usually combined with nuts (cashews, peanuts, etc.), which are yang in terms of digestion as compared to the meat. As previously mentioned, nuts contain high levels of unsaturated fatty acids and help increase HDLs (high-density lipoproteins, known as "good cholesterol"). These substances can remove the yin LDLs (low-density lipoproteins, known as "bad cholesterol") from arterial walls (a yang action). Therefore, nuts taste good with meat dishes that are high in saturated fatty acids that promote LDLs.

Dishes that contain the same ingredients may taste good in one restaurant and not good in another. The difference lies in the preparation of the foods, the proportions of the ingredients, and the cooking methods. All of these factors bring about different physiological reactions in each individual.

Conclusion

There are many factors associated with diet and food; from a food's source to its taste, temperature, smell and method of cooking. Evaluating all of these components through the principles of yin and yang will help clarify the properties of foods and help us predetermine the effects they will have on our bodies. Foods are not good or bad (with the exception of junk food) and they need to be considered in light of their effect on the body and their combination with other foods in a balanced diet.

There are two requisites to improving one's health with foods. The first is to understand who you are in terms of yin and yang, and the second is to know the yin and yang impact of various foods. Armed with such knowledge, you can accurately balance yourself with an assortment of foods suited to your yin or yang, and you will be on your way to optimal and radiant health.

CHAPTER 6
Yin and Yang of Politics

In this world no decision is ever all good or all bad. The merits of one decision may be seen as shortcomings when viewed from another perspective. This truth is the Inversion Principle at play and the nature of politics in the US.

The US government is primarily a bipartisan system reflecting the interplay between yin and yang. This type of system allows political issues to be viewed from more than one perspective often with very different interpretations. We see this constantly as Democratic policies are favored by the more liberal minded and Republican policies are favored by conservatives. However, while this is a simplistic view of a complicated system, the reality of political divisions is clearly seen when explained using the theory of yin and yang.

The term "liberal" is not necessarily synonymous with a democratic outlook and "conservative" is not always synonymous with being Republican. There are conservative Democrats and liberal Republicans. This is the principle of yin within yang and yang within yin. If Democrats are yang, liberal Democrats are yang within yang and conservative Democrats are yin within yang. Similarly, conservative Republicans are yin within yin, while liberal Republicans are yang within yin. The various demands of the times determine whether the government itself will tilt towards yin or yang, conservative or liberal, Republican or Democratic.

The policies of both the Democratic and Republican parties are actually bent on maintaining a balance. The Democratic Party is known to be pro-choice. Ultimately, this allows death (yin) to occur. On the other hand, the party is fundamentally against the death penalty, ensuring life (yang). The Republican view is just the opposite. The party is known to be pro-life (yang), which ensures more people, but is in favor of the death penalty (yin).

In regard to taxes and monetary distribution, Democrats are known to be more liberal minded (yang). However, they are generally the party responsible for tax increases and greater government regulations. These are yin actions because higher taxes centralize the distribution of wealth, while more governmental regulations restrict the actions of people in society. The taxes, however, are then put into programs attempting to equalize the distribution of wealth. This is a yang action because it is an outward and progressive form of government. Republicans are known to be more conservative (yin). They are generally in favor of lowering taxes and having fewer governmental regulations (yang). However, this allows the allocation of money to remain stratified and decentralized (yang).

The U.S. Government

The U.S. government is separated into three branches: the executive branch, which enforces the law; the legislative branch, which creates the law; and the judicial branch, which maintains the law. These different levels were devised to prevent absolute rule by any single branch of government. In terms of the *I Ching*, the three branches maintain the harmony of yin and yang.

The executive branch has many workers and layers, from the President of the United States to the police. The president has the power to veto laws passed by the legislative branch. This gives one person a great deal of power (yang). In addition, this branch of government is charged with enforcing the laws through police regulation. It is the most yang aspect of the government.

The judicial branch is an interpretive body. Decisions that are handed down by juries and local, state and federal courts are based on laws that have already been established. For example, the Supreme Court's rulings are guided by the Constitution. Such restrictions are extremely yin in nature. As this level of government does not create laws, its true power lies in interpreting laws for all citizens, including the president, to follow.

The legislative branch represents the people and has both yin and yang characteristics. Every member of this branch, as well as every member of society, must adhere to the laws of the nation. There are strict regulatory mechanisms by which laws can be passed and the people's voices heard. These mechanisms are considered yin. On the other hand, the legislative branch has the power to impeach the president and members of the Supreme Court. It thus maintains ultimate power over both the executive and judicial branches. It also has the power to create laws. In addition, even if the president were to veto a law, it could still be passed in the legislative branch. These activities are yang in nature. Because of its dual, yin-yang nature, the legislative branch is the most balanced among the three branches and is considered Tai Chi.

Capitalism versus Communism

Theoretically a country can exist in a state of either capitalism or communism (socialism). Capitalism recognizes private ownership of property and goods. Under this system the regulation of individual economic activity becomes increasingly difficult because it is very dynamic, individualistic and diffuse. This aspect of capitalism is yang. Communism suppresses individual economic activity. Economic regulations are aimed at benefiting the whole. These activities are directed inward toward a single center and are yin.

The world's governments classically follow the principles of yin and yang. The yin-yang principle of Transformation is evident in the current movement of communist governments such as Russia and the People's Republic of China toward the ideals of private property, the strength of capitalism. The reverse is occurring in the capitalistic United States. The conglomerates of big business are merging to form larger, unified entities with concentrated interests. When action diversifies to a great extent, there is a tendency to restructure. In addition, when guidelines are too stringent, there is a tendency to disperse. The capitalism and communism of the Cold War Era no longer exist. Their influences move toward one another so they become difficult to distinguish.

Morality and Politics

Political affiliation is a personal and often sensitive subject. Politics guides people's lives and is entwined with many other areas of life including religion, economics, family, morality, etc. One of the most public examples of politics meeting personal decisions came to light during the impeachment of President Clinton. Clinton's actions, however, can be better understood when analyzed using the principles of yin-yang theory.

In the East, male genitals are referred to as a "yang substance" meaning they are infused with a great deal of yang energy. The ignition of sexual desires is referred to as the "movement of yang energy." At the time of his indiscretion, Clinton was relatively young and had a great deal of power. Youth implies activity, a yang quality, and power of this nature is also yang. Morals and ethics, on the other hand, are principles that bind and impede the flow of instinctive urges and are therefore considered yin. Yang-natured people naturally dislike yin impediments. In addition, when yang energy moves in a person who already has strong yang energy, moral yin is unable to restrain it and is easily overcome. Therefore, such an individual is less likely to heed morality. Though he may exercise caution for fear of reprisal, he nevertheless will proceed with his affairs.

Clinton's indiscretions are an indication of his exceedingly yang-type personality. It can be viewed that while his actions in the Oval Office were morally reproachable, his yang nature was nationally beneficial.

Economics, like politics, is intimately tied to morality and ethics. A state of economic depression is yin while economic growth is yang. In order to activate or revitalize a depressed economy (yin), it is best to have a yang-natured person as president. Only a yang-natured individual has the ability to overcome sluggish yin and revitalize the economy. A person who is excessively yin and overly concerned with morals could never accomplish this. George Bush, Sr., who was greatly concerned with his moral appearance, was unable to restore the country to economic health. In contrast, President Clinton, who tested America's moral standards, managed to get the country's economy back on track. According to these principles, the economy would see larger gains under a liberal administration (though not necessarily Democratic), and would tend to be depressed under a conservative rule.

Fortunately for President Clinton, there is a connection between having liberal morals and inciting a strong economy. Americans seem to place greater value on economic revival than on the indiscretions of their president. If this were not the case, Clinton's impeachment proceedings may have run a different course. Most people will forgive (or at least ignore) indiscretions while their bank accounts are growing. During periods of economic prosperity, people are actually more likely to commit immoral acts as they look for interesting and unusual ways to spend their newfound wealth. Recall, for example, the prosperity of the "Roaring 20s" and its correspondingly high crime rates.

Eventually, however, yang will transform into yin. The *I Ching* states, "Extreme yang produces yin and extreme yin produces yang." Abundant economic life generates activity, and excessive activity (yang) is bound to transgress even the most sacred restraint (yin). When this happens, social problems crop up until they finally reach the forefront of public consciousness. Once the excitement of economic revival is replaced by stability and comfort, people's minds return to issues of morality. The resurgence of morality generally slows activity and economic decline begins again.

There are indicators of stages of yin-yang development in nature as well as in society. A popular saying in the stock market is that the state of economy can be known by the hemline of skirts at any given time. More specifically, the rise of hemlines indicates economic revival and the popularity of long skirts indicates economic depression. This may seem outrageous, but by applying the principles of yin and yang, the connection becomes apparent. Economic revival (yang) is accompanied by more freedom and activity, while economic depression (yin) means more restraint and a greater emphasis on morality. Indicators, such as skirt length, are referred to as "images" in the *I Ching*.

Politicians could greatly improve their governing abilities if they were to analyze these images and use them to determine whether the current of the times was flowing towards yin or yang. It is also important for them to understand whether their own nature belongs to yin or yang and to cultivate their weaknesses. In ancient eastern politics, those who did not understand yin-yang and the *I Ching* were considered children in the political world, incapable of governing effectively. Theories of the *I Ching* were also studied and utilized by more modern political thinkers such as Chairman Mao and Karl Marx.

CHAPTER 7
Yin and Yang of the Economy

The material (yin) and energetic (yang) aspects of the economy are rooted in the interchange and exchange of money (yin) and labor (yang). Money is considered yin because it is tangible, stored energy. Labor or work is yang because it involves activity of the body or mind regardless of whether it is blue collar (yang) or white collar (yin). Like everything else in the universe, the material (yin) and energetic (yang) aspects of the economy are constantly transforming into one another. Work and labor (yang) are converted into money (yin) when people are financially compensated for their work. Money can then be converted back into work and labor when it is used to pay people for their efforts. Viewed in this way we see that work is the energy and money is the substance of the economy. Work transforming into money and back into work is similar to yin transforming into yang and back to yin.

In the body, surplus energy is stored as fat. When needed, fats are transformed into carbohydrates, which may then be converted into ATP (the energy unit of the body) and used to contract muscles (or do work). Similarly, surplus energy from labor is converted into money and stored in the bank (or some other safe location). When needed, money is used and there is a transfer of energy.

One of the most basic principles of economics is the law of supply and demand. When there is a need for a product or service (demand), a person able to fill the need (supply) should reap the benefits of his or her labor–the greater the need, the greater the benefit. Demand is considered to be yin because it calls for the reception of goods, whereas supply is yang because it involves the sending out of goods. When there is more supply (yang) than demand (yin), prices go down; when there is more demand (yin) than supply (yang), prices go up. An excess of either yin or yang will create its opposite. An excessive supply (yang) will make prices drop (yin), and an excessive demand (yin) will create higher prices (yang). Falling prices are considered yin because they contract, whereas rising prices are thought to be yang because they expand or inflate.

Some people work all their lives and do not accumulate wealth, while others may inherit great sums of money and never have to work. A young person who inherits money obviously did not have to work very hard to acquire his or her wealth. The inheritance, however, did not develop by itself. At some point effort was made to amass the wealth. Once effort is in a yin form, it is easily transferred from one person to another.

Another factor that comes into play is the psychological and social stresses that may accompany the intake of money. Illegal, high-risk work tends to be more highly paid than a similar legal occupation. Dealing drugs, for example, is a highly stressful and dangerous job. The social and legal restrictions on selling drugs give higher value to the product, because more effort is required to make and distribute or in many cases smuggle the drugs, than would be necessary if the drugs were legal. In addition, the social stresses that fall on the people involved in the process contribute to the perceived worth of the drugs.

Making easy money by selling drugs does not mean that the person did not do much work. Rather, dealers are given large lump payments for their emotional and potentially physical suffering. To avoid being caught, dealers have to endure significant amounts of stress or tension. Illegal or dangerous work takes great toll physically, mentally and emotionally in a short amount of time compared to legal jobs which can also be highly stressful but not to the degree of illegal activities. In addition, the self-value of criminals was bought cheaply and they suffer personal shame and public disgrace, as well as insult and slandering from others. Eventually they can end up in a jail or be shot and be killed. Thus their money was not easily earned.

Another stressful occupation is prostitution. Here, the shame and disgrace prostitutes suffer is much greater than they would from other jobs. At first glance it appears that prostitutes make a great deal of money for very little work. However, the shame she feels is several hundred times more than she would feel if her job involved cleaning dishes or a bathroom. The more fortitude required to succeed in an occupation and the more abuse (real or potential) a person may endure as a result of "professional hazards," the more money that can be made in a short span of time.

Doctors and lawyers are paid more money per hour than plumbers or electricians because the number of hours of training and education doctors and lawyers undergo is higher than the training requirements for plumbers and electricians. When all of the factors are taken into account, the reasons for the disparity in wages are easier to understand thus reducing the need to be envious of how others earn money. The money (yin) one makes is directly proportional to the degree of effort and suffering one endures while working (yang). A business executive may earn more money than an employee. However, he or she must take on much greater responsibility thereby using (yang) or expending (yang) a tremendous amount of mental energy.

The rules of yin and yang also apply to money acquired by chance, such as from the Lotto or Las Vegas slot machines. In these situations, there is the possibility of winning a large sum of money in an instant and everyone is given, more or less, the same odds of winning. If you toss a coin a thousand times, the chance of landing on heads or tails is equal every time. Fortune and misfortune in a person's life are similarly dispensed. In addition, fortune (yang) is always associated with a price (yin) and misfortune (yin) with some form of progress (yang).

Most people consider it a misfortune not to have a lot of money. They feel depressed because they do not seem to be making enough money in proportion to the amount of work they do. Having a proper yin-yang perspective can reduce the suffering for these people. The reason people do not earn enough money is that they do not work hard enough. People must work hard physically and constantly administer to the direction of their business. They need to mentally prepare for changes that may arise in the future. The ability to predict the future of one's business is based on extensive knowledge that can only be gained by investing a great deal of effort and learning lessons through trial and error. People must read books, ask experts and experience failure so they can learn from their mistakes rather than blaming their misfortune on economic tides.

Success does not necessarily equal wealth. However, economically successful people work hard–either physically or mentally–to convert their work into money, irrespective of their luck. In prosperous times they work hard and save their earnings instead of spending irresponsibly. In bad times they continue to work hard, using setbacks as learning experiences to improve their future performance.

Applying Yin and Yang to the Stock Market

Let's suppose, for example, you are a fund manager in the stock market. Your major concern is the rise and fall of stock prices. Yang is a rise in prices and yin is a downturn. Determining the time at which these may occur is Tai Chi. The diagram below represents the trend of prices (Fig. 7.1). A through B represents the rise in prices after a fall. Points B through C represent the time when prices are rising. C through D represents the fall in prices after a period of increase. And D through E is when prices are bottoming out.

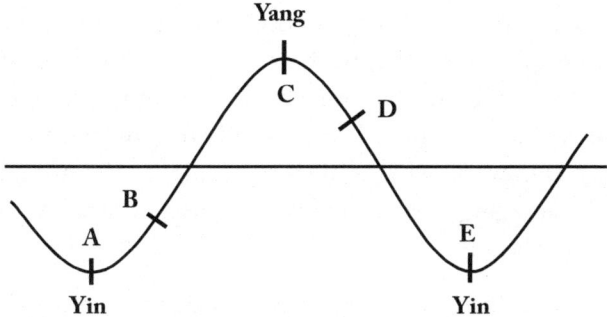

Figure 7.1 Yin-Yang of the Stock Market

The factors that affect stock market prices can be divided and classified into yin and yang. Factors that raise the prices are yang, and those that lower prices are yin. Those can be further broken down into immediate results and long term results. For instance, something that raises the prices on the market immediately is yang when compared to something with a slower result. In this example, the rise in stock prices (yang) is Tai Chi and the speed of the effect on the market is broken down into yin and yang. This can be applied to yin as well. The result is a spectrum of yin and yang to help determine when might be a good time to invest. Once these trends are defined, the prices of the changing market can be compared to the changing patterns of *I Ching*, and you may be able to predict the changes in the stock market.

CHAPTER 8
Yin and Yang of Perspective

Differences in perspectives and perceptions are the root of many conflicts and misunderstandings. Confucius said, "If you do not have it in your mind, you will not see or hear it." Every visual object, sound, smell, taste and feeling we perceive, we relate to past experience in order to interpret and understand the sensation. If we hear a sound that we have never heard before, we would have to investigate its origin in order to conceptualize what it comes from. The same is true of thoughts and ideation. If a person is not aware of the existence of something, they cannot conceive of it. For example, we did not know there was a possibility of damaging the ozone layer of the atmosphere until we knew there was an ozone layer.

Anything viewed with a yang expectation will appear more yin. Conversely, anything viewed with a yin expectation will appear more yang. The scandal surrounding President Clinton's term in office is an example of people in high places with high expectations from the public. People in high positions have a greater distance to fall. The mistakes made by those who are most respected are greatly amplified. This is in sharp contrast to events that surround the lives of those who do not hold public office.

In Korea doctors, lawyers and judges all have the honorific character for "teacher" at the end of their titles. At the same time, the people who hold these jobs are sometimes referred to as "licensed thieves." When we expect the world from people (yang), anything they do wrong will appear like a crime (yin). We have high expectations from famous people, thus even a minor offense is blown out of proportion. On the other hand, when we have fewer expectations from people (yin), their actions can seem great (yang). This is an example of how yang constantly changes into yin and yin into yang, in the material world and in reasoning.

It all boils down to expectations—or more specifically, perspectives. Most of us have been educated on the so-called "truths" determined by scholars and scientists. We believe that we live on Earth, which is but a small part of the solar system, which is in turn a small part of the Milky Way, which is in turn a small part of the infinite universe. We classify ourselves as "organisms" when we consider the duality between organic and inorganic matter. We classify ourselves as "animal" when we consider the duality between plants and animals. Among the group "animal," we consider ourselves part of the subset "mammal," and so on. From our egocentric perspectives we believe that we are able to observe the natural world with clarity, but we are unaware of the filter of our preconceived notions. We stand before a fire and think how strong the flames are, forgetting that in relation to the sun, the fire is not so hot. In this way we lose perspective, allowing our daily problems to encompass our thoughts. We are not looking at the bigger picture.

The following eastern anecdote called "Weeping Lady" aptly illustrates how our self-limiting perspective can cause turmoil in life:

> There was an old woman who had two sons. The older son sold umbrellas for a living while the younger son maintained a salt farm. The old woman was constantly crying, worrying about her sons' lots in life. On sunny days, the old lady cried because she worried that her older son's umbrella business would fail. On rainy days, she cried because she was afraid that her younger son's salt farm would be damaged.
>
> One day, a passing monk took pity on the old woman. The monk told the old woman she should be happy on sunny days because the salt farm will fair well and she should be happy on rainy days because the umbrella business will fair well. From that day forward, the old lady changed her frame of mind and was happy.

A Perspective on Medicines of East and West

Easterners created eastern medicine, and though it differs radically from western medicine, it has as its subject the same human body. Neither view is more correct than the other; they are simply different interpretations of the same structures and functioning.

The ancient sages who founded eastern medicine drew the internal organs in an abstract, idealistic manner and spoke of the physiology of the organs in a different way. They were not "wrong" or "inaccurate," rather they emphasized a different aspect of the organs. Eastern doctors were obviously acquainted with the internal organs. They conducted cadaver and animal dissections. Nevertheless, they drew and spoke of the organs' structures and physiology in a completely different way because they operated from a different mode of thinking or reasoning. Their innate perspectives were derived from different experiences, teachings and observational points of view.

Seeing the Big Picture

Experiments conducted within the realm of the scientific method purport to be free of interpretation. However, whenever there is a human being involved in either administrating or analyzing data, there is a level of subjectivity that exists. Perhaps this is the final experiment leading to the conclusion of a book that the experimenter has taken ten years to complete. The results of the experiment determine whether or not the work will be published. The findings most definitely will adhere to the hypothesis of the experiment. There is also great competition to establish funding for experimentation and the results can be interpreted in more than one way depending on the desired outcome. This is not to say that pure scientific research is not without merit. We must keep in mind the human element in every situation. In scientific research, as in daily life, the observational viewpoint varies greatly. The psychological state of the observer greatly determines what information is absorbed and how that information is interpreted.

The reasoning of yin-yang theory allows investigation to occur from the viewpoint of the observer while maintaining the perspective of the whole. It does, however, leave room for bias in its calculations. A person well versed in yin-yang reasoning would claim that a fire is strong only after carefully comparing all things in nature or the universe to the fire. This system of calculations would be as follows: within the universe, in our solar system, on Earth, among organisms, between fire (yang) and water (yin)–fire is hotter (yang). The degree of strength of the fire can also be classified according to the principle of Infinite Divisibility of the yin-yang equation. There is yin within yang and yang within yin. Using this method of comparison, the strength of the fire is put into perspective.

Analog and Digital Analysis

The reasoning process of yin-yang theory is, in one respect, identical to the process a computer uses to recognize data. A computer "thinks" in a digital mode rather than in analog. Analog is a method of interpreting data by comparison. An analog clock face has hands rather than simply displaying numbers. By looking at an analog clock we are able to see how the seconds, minutes and hours relate to one another. A digital clock face tells the precise time, but does not show how one moment relates to the five before or the ten after. Analog indicators function by comparison. When buying stocks, it is not enough to know the price of the stock. A good investor would want an analog comparison of the price of a stock for reference.

Both analog and digital methods of analysis have their strengths and weaknesses. While analog allows for comparison, digital can be more exact. The digital mode is superior in clarifying random and confusing situations into logical order, but it does not give a complete and holistic view of things. The yin and yang mode of reasoning allows a person to switch from analog to digital and vice versa. This means that it allows both inductive and deductive reasoning.

This is the beauty of yin and yang. It gives a holistic view that illuminates the relationships between things, and at the same time, it gives an analytical and detailed view of any situation. Yin and yang together show the whole picture as well as close ups of each part. This method of reasoning can help eliminate the observer's preconceived notions and allow a more complete understanding of all things in nature.

The following are diagrams of an Analog Tai Chi and a Digital Tai Chi (Figure 8.1). You can see that in the analog Tai Chi, the boundaries between each color are unclear and seem to blend together. In the Digital Tai Chi, however, there is a clear and distinct boundary, distinguishing the two representative colors of yin and yang.

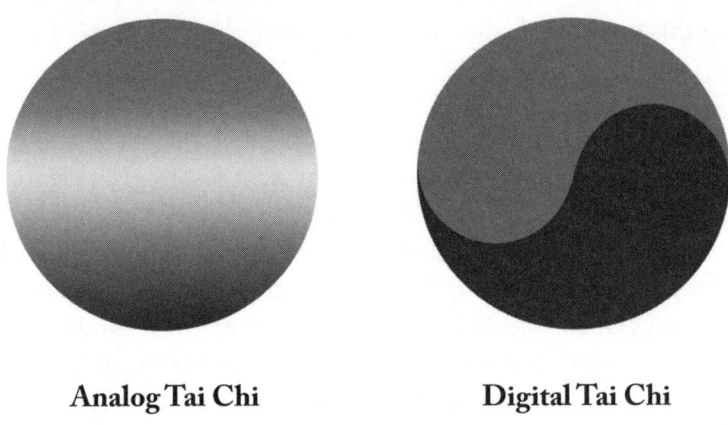

Analog Tai Chi   **Digital Tai Chi**

Figure 8.1 Analog and Digital Tai Chi

CHAPTER 9
Yin and Yang of Music

Music is a universal language that can truly gather and unite people. This is echoed in the popular phrase, "The family that sings together stays together." It embodies the principles of yin and yang more clearly than anything else because music can be a source not only of joy, pleasure and healing (all yang qualities) but also of sorrow, fear, sickness and terror (all yin qualities). Music can bring about peace and tranquility as well as confusion and chaos. It is the most profound form of expression humans create. Can you think of a television show, radio program, commercial, movie, or Broadway show that does not have music?

We hear music everywhere, whether it is during the holiday season, at an inauguration, graduation or commencement, or simply at a party. In nature we hear the chirping of birds or cicadas, the rustling of leaves and the sounds of a stream or river. Life would be exceptionally dull, monotonous and boring in the absence of the melodic variations between passion and peace or excitement and tranquility. In fact, nothing in this universe would exist without music. Music is life itself, and without it no life can exist.

Influence of Music

Sounds affect people's minds. Music with a high pitch and fast tempo can excite people, while music with a low pitch and slow tempo can mellow them. By attuning the frequency, tone and tempo of sound to the theory of the *I Ching*, beautiful music can develop. This can be accomplished by alternating sounds that have a high pitch and fast tempo with those that have a low pitch and slow tempo, or by combining sounds that have a low pitch and fast tempo with those that have a high pitch and slow tempo. When there is no order to the pitch (high/low) or tempo (fast/slow), it is perceived as noise.

Human physiology resonates according to the principles of the universe. Noise impedes the natural processes of human physiology and is therefore harmful. People are naturally repelled by this type of noise. Listening to beautiful music, however, harmoniously promotes human physiology. People are naturally attracted to this type of music and will pay high admission prices to hear it performed live. Beautiful sounds that have a similar frequency to human physiology are the sounds of life (yang) because they facilitate physiological processes. Noise, is the sound of death (yin), because it impedes normal human physiological processes.

The direct influence of music is shown by its influence on plant life. People are familiar with the concept of talking to and playing music for plants to help them grow. There are numerous reports about the accelerated growth of plants that are showered with beautiful music.[1] If you play noise and try to grow plants, they will not grow well; flowers will not blossom, and trees will have a difficult time bearing fruit. Though smog might contribute to making trees wither on a busy city street, the noise from the traffic is also a significant factor.

There have also been numerous studies regarding the development and intelligence of children related to musical influence. There have been reports of higher IQs in children born to women who played Baroque music for them while they were in the womb. A recent report from China states that for children less than six years old, listening to Mozart may increase their IQ levels. Aside from increasing children's IQ levels, Mozart's music has also been known to increase the milk flow of cows in Brittany, France, and quell drug trafficking in Edmonton, Canada.[2]

Music Therapy

Creating music influenced by a thorough study of how sounds affect the human body and mind would be like developing a new drug to treat specific ailments. It would be possible to treat not only psychological disorders but also certain organic diseases. "Music therapy" already exists in the East and West. There are many CDs available which address specific problems such as headaches, pain, and depression.

YIN AND YANG OF MUSIC

There are two ways in which music can induce healing. The first is by vibrating the eardrum to stimulate the brain. When music vibrates the eardrum, sound changes into electrical signals that are transmitted to the brain. The brain interprets the signals and creates sensations or emotions which cause bodily reactions by way of the nervous and endocrine systems. The other way music affects the body is by resonating directly with molecules or cells in order to stimulate physiological processes.

Diseases arise out of an imbalance of yin and yang. The purpose of human physiological processes is to maintain a dynamic balance. Yin and yang fluctuate up and down within certain parameters. Sometimes yin is greater than yang and other times yang is greater than yin. While these two elements are in constant flux, when there is a continued excess of yin without the recovery of yang or vice versa, disease occurs.

Music with a yin nature can activate the yin functions of the human body. For yang-type diseases (which are due to the excessive excitation of sympathetic nerves) where a person is emotionally excited or has a fever, headache, a fast pulse, and high blood pressure, stimulating the yin functions (excitation of parasympathetic nerves) will balance yin and yang to treat these diseases. Likewise, yang-type music can be applied to treat yin-type diseases in which a person has a cold body, pain, coldness in the abdomen, a slow pulse, and low blood pressure. By listening to yang-natured music when yang is not recovering or to yin-natured music when yin is not recovering, yin and yang will return to a balanced state and healing will take place.

In Korea, healing is done with musical instruments in several ways. For example, people who are suffering from stomach ailments, such as indigestion and stomachaches, or bowel problems, such as constipation or Crohn's disease, are treated with the sounds of drums. Drums are hollow and covered with an animal skin. This is similar to the constitution of the bowels. Therefore, the sounds of drums resonate the whole abdominal cavity, bringing it back to a balanced state. Headaches are treated by playing a small gong, a percussion instrument made of metal. The sounds made by a gong resonate with the cells of the brain, making them reverberate in a synchronized fashion. This action not only helps eliminate headaches, but also helps people focus or concentrate. The Korean archers are renowned for their accuracy. They have consistently won gold medals in the Olympics and other international competitions. They are well known for practicing their events surrounded by the loud sounds made by the gong.

These are examples of treating specific ailments with music. But there are other things music can do. For instance, diseases of society can be treated with music. Playing music that is balanced in yin-yang will harmonize and settle people's minds. Can a person develop thoughts of stealing while he is listening to holy music majestically played with a pipe organ in a cathedral? When you watch a movie and something is about to happen, music with an unbalanced tone and rhythm plays in the background. This causes people to become unsettled and anxious. There is an abrupt change in the high and low tones as well as a sudden change in the tempo. The balance of yin and yang is broken explicitly to elicit feelings of anxiety, fear, confusion and chaos. Try turning down the sound on a scary movie and feel how your apprehensions fade. If this type of unbalanced music becomes popular, society may become disordered and fall into a state of confusion. But if yin-yang balanced music becomes popular, society can become stable and orderly.

The Sounds of Society

The dynamic nature of American society is reflected in its popular music. Today's popular music resonates with a greater yang frequency, adding to the momentum of society. If we were to analyze all of the music played in American culture in terms of pitch and tone, we would probably find a 60:40 ratio of yang to yin music because of the predominance of rap music. Many young people like gangster rap, which has a strong beat. It is a yang form of music that resonates with young people who by nature are yang. However, because rap music is so yang, it can over stimulate the yang functioning of the body and lead to an imbalance. Nevertheless, much of the popular rap music has a relative yin and yang balance. The songs begin with a strong sense of tension (yang) that resembles a battlefield and then a female voice (yin) appears. This shows that even in a push toward the extreme, there is always an opposing force attempting to reestablish the relative harmony of yin and yang. This is the homeostatic mechanism of Tai Chi.

We can gain insight into someone's personality by understanding the nature of the music he or she chooses to listen to. This may seem an obvious point, but once we have a better understanding of the nature of yin and yang, knowledge of what may stimulate a person can lead to a greater understanding of many other aspects of that person. Older adults have a greater likelihood of listening to classical or country music. Classical music is yin-yang balanced music, whereas country music is generally yin-type music. These two forms of music relate well to the yin nature of mature age. People with strong religious convictions tend to enjoy religious music, which is often times yin in nature. This, too, is a reflection of people's physiological state. Moreover, by listening to the music of a certain time period or a certain region, we can gain an understanding of the conditions and trends of that society.

Yin and Yang of Instruments

The lower the pitch an instrument produces, the more yin it is; the higher the pitch, the more yang. Among wind instruments, the tuba is the most yin and the piccolo is the most yang. Among stringed instruments the double bass is most yin and the violin is the most yang. Percussion instruments have a wide variety of sounds. Among them, the sounds of the bass drum are the most yin and those of the triangle are the most yang. The piano may be considered a percussion instrument because it creates sounds by percussing tight strings. It has the most balanced yin and yang characteristics of any instrument. It is said that the sound produced by playing the central key of a piano has the same tone as the cry of a newborn baby.

The tone of an instrument determines its yin or yang classification, and within each instrument there may be further divisions of yin and yang depending on the notes played. When instruments combine to play a structured mixture of high and low tones as well as long and short rhythms, they create harmonious sounds. This is an example of the divisions of yin and yang within everything. Just as all things that have different tilts of yin and yang gather together to compose the universe, and cells with different tilts of yin and yang form a human being, so too can rhythms and tones with different tilts of yin and yang gather to make balanced, orchestral music.

The Power of Music

Napoleon's army is said to have gone to battle with marching music. This type of music helped raise fortitude and a fighting spirit to the highest degree. It helped set the right tone so that fear and hesitation melted away from the minds and bodies of his men. Actually, playing music during battle was a technique used frequently in the East. Armies of the East were led to attack with the sound of a gong and retreat with the sound of drums. At times they used high-pitched timbre-like instruments to confuse and bring chaos to their enemies.

The influence of yin and yang music on a society and its people is quite strong. Masters of the East who understood this principle heavily emphasized the study of music. *Yul Ryuh*, reflections on music as interpreted by the *I Ching*, is considered to be the highest form of study and meditation in the East. In modern terms, *Yul Ryuh* is the study of vibrational waves and frequencies. The classics of the East are studied in a certain order with the *Yul Ryuh* as the final chapter.

With a good understanding of the principles of *Yul Ryuh*, it is possible to synchronize the frequency of the mind, body and spirit with that of the Tao through the frequency of music. This is what happens in chanting. It is also the nature of the power of authority that music can have. People's minds can be influenced by resonation. Recall the last time you unexpectedly heard a song from your childhood. Music has the power to elicit strong feelings and emotions. It can influence the psychological aspects of the human mind as well as physical aspects of the human body. It can be used to harm as well as to heal.

The powerful influence of music can be seen not only on a personal level but also through the existence and continuity of an entire state or nation. In the East, when a new dynasty comes into power a *Hwang Jong*, or Golden Bell, is immediately made. *Hwang Jong* is a bell that produces the most balanced tone in music, like the central key of the piano. All musicians tune their instruments to the *Hwang Jong*. During ancient times in the East the *Hwang Jong* was made to produce a perfectly balanced sound with 50:50 proportions of yin and yang. If the pitch tilted to either yin or yang, even slightly, the country was considered to be unbalanced, leading to chaos and the downfall of the dynasty.

YIN AND YANG OF MUSIC

The Pied Piper is another famous tale that resonates with the same yin-yang principles. The power of the Piper's flute was that it was in tune with the balanced pitch of the Golden Bell. Rats, animals and children would follow him because of its perfect pitch. If it were not in tune, they would not have been drawn to the sound. The *Hwang Jong* of ancient dynasties is like the flute of the Piper.

CHAPTER 10
Yin and Yang of Wave

Everything in the universe is comprised of matter that has visible forms, and energy that has no visible form. Regardless of how small matter is split, it is always divided into two parts—matter and energy. Matter can be measured by its mass, while energy can be known by its wave pattern.

Just as yin transforms into yang and yang into yin, matter (yin) changes into energy (yang) and vice versa. Matter has a tendency to transform into energy, while energy has a tendency to turn into matter. When matter transforms into energy, it appears as wave. Not only are the compositions of all things in the universe made up of two components known as yin and yang, but so are their movements. The way in which the movements manifest is by an alternation of a strong and a weak emission of energy in a wave pattern (Fig. 10.1).

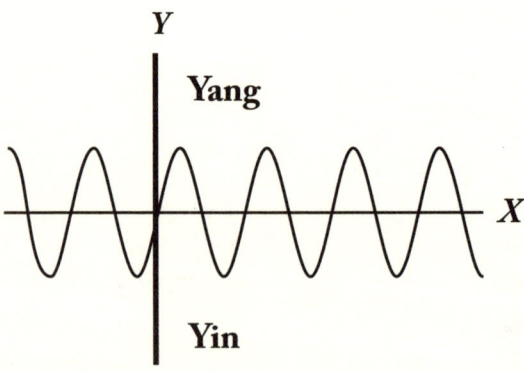

Figure 10.1 Movements of All Things in the Universe

YIN AND YANG OF WAVE

Ultimately, a wave is alternating occurrence of yin and yang. When the X coordinate that represents time is added to the Y coordinate, which expresses strength (yang) and weakness (yin) of energy, the wave can be described in such a graph. All things that have movement have such wave form. For instance, the Earth rotates around its axis and revolves around the sun. By rotating about its axis, it fluctuates between yin and yang of day and night according to the time. By revolving around the sun, it alternately repeats winter and summer according to the flow of time. According to such iteration of yin and yang, all human beings live and their pulses change. During the daytime and the summer, which belong to yang, the pulse speeds up, while during the night and the winter, which belong to yin, the pulse slows down. When the changes of yin and yang in these three aspects are shown in a diagram it appears as follows (Fig.10.2):

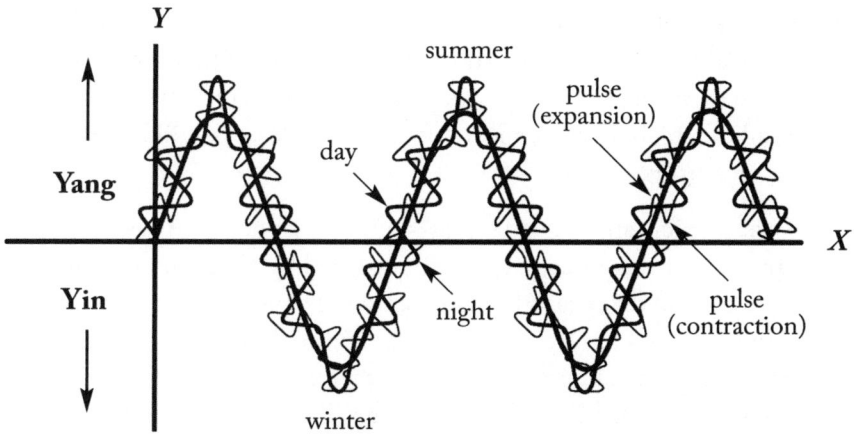

Figure 10.2 Change in the Pulse According to Seasons

Just as there are yin-yang within yin and yin-yang within yang in the composition of the all things in the universe, there are yin-yang within yin and yin-yang within yang in their movements. This is clearly shown in the diagram. Just as all matters in the universe are expressed according to the variance of their yin and yang, the wave is that which expresses yin and yang of energy flow according to variance of yin and yang. Therefore, both the constituent components, which are the substantial aspect of everything in the universe and the wave, which is the energetic aspect, can be classified according to the variance of yin and yang.

Waves are classified according to the number of changes of yin and yang that take place within a second. The greater change, the more yin the wave is, while the fewer changes indicate a yang wave. This is due to classifying the yin and yang of energy and not of matter. Since the viewpoint has turned 180 degrees, i.e., the Inversion Principle, the standard of yin and yang changes. When classifying constituent components that are still the faster movements imply yang, but when classifying energies, which are dynamic, the faster movements indicate yin. Therefore, the energy of a wave that has higher frequency becomes yin, while lower frequency wave becomes yang.

Since everything in the universe has both substantial and energetic elements, human beings can recognize them through either material or energetic aspects. Individual objects have a particular sound or color and sounds and colors can be recognized as energetic waves. Those waves of energy that are beyond the measuring range of our senses such as ultrasound, infrared rays, gamma rays and x-rays, all of which do not appear as sound or color, can still be recognized by utilizing measuring instruments.

The waves, which are recognized as sound or color, are measured by the sense organs such as ears or eyes and then analyzed by the human brain. Those waves that are beyond the measuring range of sense organs so that measuring instruments must be used to recognize them can be analyzed through computers, which correspond to the human brain, in order to recognize their particular characteristics. At such time if the yin and yang of wave based on the analytical standards of the computer is applied, then the information of yin and yang of that matter can be known. This implies that by measuring the wave of the matter through the measuring instrument that contains a program of analyzing yin and yang, the particular nature of the matter, whether yin or yang, can be known.

CHAPTER 11
Yin and Yang of the Universe

Yin	Yang
Matter	Energy
Proton	Electron
Particle	Wave
Qi (energy)	Li (organizing principle)
Long wave	Short wave
Black Hole	White Hole

Table 11.1 Yin-Yang of the Universe

The universe is composed of matter and energy, yin and yang. Yin relates to the substantive aspect or the ability to hold form, while yang is the energetic aspect or the ability to enact change. Another way of looking at yin and yang is that yin is the physical body while yang is the mind or mental functioning. This division is obvious when we look at human beings. However, when we look at the mind for what it truly is, a compilation of energetic guiding principles, we understand that even inorganic substances have primitive minds.

In human beings the body is substance and the mind is energy. The mind controls and regulates the body, while the body houses and nourishes the mind. But let's look at a piece of granite. Granite is composed of mica, feldspar and quartz. If we further breakdown feldspar, we are left with one silicon atom and two oxygen atoms. A silicon atom (like all atoms) consists of a nucleus (a "solid" substance) and electrons (orbiting particles of energy).

According to the theory of yin and yang, the solid nucleus is yin and the external active electrons are yang. In addition, we know that yin and yang are constantly dividing into smaller and smaller parts. Regardless of how small subatomic particles may be, they can always be further divided. Following this reasoning, whenever there is substance (yin), there must also be an energetic component (yang). So, whenever there is a body (yin) there must also be a mind (yang).

Looking back at our example, the substantive aspect of the granite is the "body" and the energetic aspect is its "mind." This mind allows the granite to interact with and respond to external stimuli, such as gravity and electromagnetic and nuclear forces.

Energy and Matter

The differences we see in nature are caused by "essential energy" taking on various shapes according to the flow of time, similar to ocean waves responding to tidal and climate changes. Influenced by external forces, such as the sun's energy, electromagnetic waves, gravity, cosmic rays, etc., this energetic medium momentarily holds a form. It can take the shape of anything as determined by the nature of the relationship of its component particles to their surrounding forces.

As Einstein proved in his theory of relativity ($E=mc^2$) and the fourth principle of yin and yang describes, energy is constantly changing into matter and matter into energy–yin to yang and back again. If we were to perceive things as they truly exist, nothing would be solid and nothing would be stationary. For example, if the elementary particles that form all substance are nothing more than vibrating energy, then there is no real difference between energy and matter.

Although a rock appears solid, it is composed of atoms, which are almost entirely empty space. This is the reason why short-wave radiation, like x-rays, can penetrate solid matter. If we split the nucleus of an atom, we would find elementary subatomic particles (yin) that are nothing more than oscillating fields of energy (yang). The reason we can see them is that they are oscillating at such a high rate that they appear to be solid particles much the same way a spinning pinwheel appears solid (Fig. 11.1).

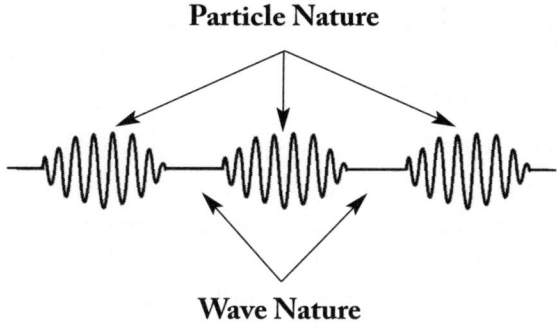

Figure 11.1 Wave and Particle

Qi (Vital Energy) and Li (Organizing Principle)

Eastern scholars who studied yin and yang called the vibrational energy "Qi" and the organizing principle "Li" (pronounced 'lee'). It is the combination of Qi and Li that creates all things in the universe. If you consider Qi as water, then Li is the container. If Li is a mug, then the Qi will conform to the shape of a mug. If Li is a bottle, then the Qi will conform to the shape of a bottle. At the level of quantum physics, Li is the force of attraction that binds energy into particles and particles into matter and Qi is the particles that succumb to the attraction.

In Buddhism it is said that, "All that exists is the same as that which does not exist." A substance that has color and can be observed is the same as that which does not have any form. And that which does not have any form is believed to be the same as a substance that has color and can be seen. These statements imply that all matter with its multifarious colors and shapes is ultimately vibrations of energy and does not truly have form. Conversely, there are imperceptible vibrations of energy within the vast emptiness of space without color or form.

Studies carried out by eastern scholars throughout the ages as to the true nature of the universe were as intense and profound as current studies into the nature of subatomic particles conducted by quantum physicists. The difference lies in the methodology. Quantum physics is actually on the road to proving what theorists of the East have known for eons. Confucian scholars made attempts to study yin and yang in a rational, "scientific" manner. Taoists and Buddhist monks, however, attempted to discover the true nature of the universe through intuition and meditation.

Quantum physics explains that subatomic particles have the dual nature of being both a particle and a wave. The wave characteristic is yang and the particle nature is yin. The famous "Double Slit" experiment in particle physics demonstrated that a particle of light is actually capable of integrating information about its surrounding and acting according to that information. In the experiment, light is made to pass through a piece of paper with two slits and onto a screen. When the experiment is done with only one slit exposed, the light spreads out evenly. When both slits are exposed, the light lands in certain alternating light and dark intervals because of interference patterns (the interaction of wave patterns). The reason this experiment became famous is that when it was done using only a single photon (particle of light) the results were the same even though there was no interference. The photons appeared to "know" where they were expected to go and reacted to their surroundings. This implies a degree of consciousness, even at the most elemental level. Yin-yang theory explains this by stating that regardless of the phenomenon, there is always a yin aspect and a yang aspect, matter and energy.

Mind and Body: Manifestation of Yin and Yang

We have just explained the reasons subatomic particles have both a mind and a body. Following this reasoning and because everything in the universe, animate and inanimate, is composed of these little "thinking" things, then everything must have both a mind and a body. The difference is the complexity or simplicity of the controlling mind. Organisms have minds that are complicated and well developed, whereas inanimate objects have minds that are simple and more primitive. Regardless of the complexity, however, every mind communicates with the mind of the universe, in the same way that all the water on the surface of the Earth connects with the boundless sea and the energy from a power plant is transmitted to the night light in a child's room.

"Thinking" subatomic particles gather to form atoms. Atoms combine to form molecules and molecules form cells. Cells unite to form tissues in the human body and these tissues form our organs. Because all of these structures are composed of subatomic particles, the functioning of our organs and all of our bodies' systems depend on the unification of their mental aspect. This unified mind is connected to the brain through nerves, and the substantial aspect of each tissue connects to the physical body through the structures of the body's systems, such as the circulatory, digestive, reproductive, and nervous systems. What we consider to be the mind is actually an integration of the mental aspects of all of the individual constituent components. The body is an integrated system of the substantial and physical aspects of these components.

From the eastern perspective, the mental and physical aspects of animals, plants and minerals combine to make up the Earth. The mental and physical aspects of individual stars combine to make up the mind and body of the universe. And the mind of the universe is Tao or Tai Chi.

Black Holes versus White Holes

The movement of the universe is a perpetual succession of birth or production (yang) and death or destruction (yin). The Quasar or White Hole (yang) generates birth, and the Black Hole (yin) is responsible for death. The manifestation of the White Hole is the Big Bang, and the manifestation of the Black Hole is the absorption of everything, even light.

At the end of the Black Hole is the White Hole. Stars that have been sucked into the Black Hole contract and ultimately explode out the other end from the White Hole. This action is known as the Big Bang. All of the substances that expand because of this explosion gradually lose speed and slowly get sucked back into the Black Hole. These substances contract and explode out again, and thus the cycle continues. When we illustrate this process, it looks like figure 11.2.

Yin and Yang of Life

Figure 11.2 Black and White Holes

The following diagram is an enlarged drawing of above diagram in regards to both Black and White Holes (Fig. 11.3).

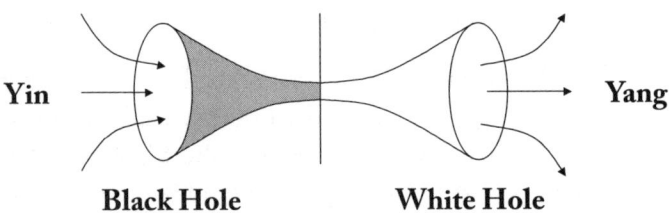

Figure 11.3 Black and White Holes Enlarged

As matter gets sucked into the Black Hole, it makes a spiraling motion, similar to the spiral movement of a ball bearing dropped into a funnel or water in a drain. When matter explodes out of or is ejected from the White Hole, it also makes a spiraling motion. This motion is the motive force behind the rotation and revolution of stars and galaxies.

YIN AND YANG OF THE UNIVERSE

The Black Hole is the ultimate yin and is associated with a negative charge. The White Hole is the ultimate yang and is associated with a positive charge. These positive and negative charges are reflected in the north and south magnetic poles of the Earth (Fig. 11.4). Its electromagnetic field is shaped like the model of the universe formed by the Black and the White Holes.

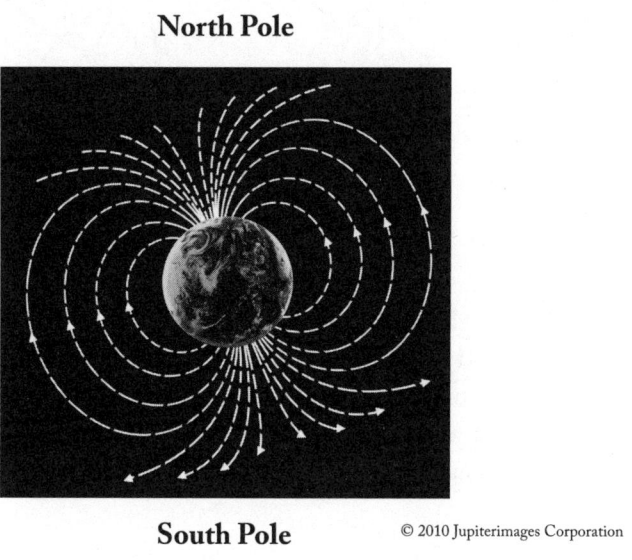

Figure 11.4 Earth's Magnetic Field

The principles governing Black and White Holes and the yin and yang of the universe can also be applied to common, everyday substances. For instance, we can measure the voltage of an egg at the ends of its major axes. This indicates that there is a positive (expanding) and negative (contracting) force in an egg. It is even possible to measure a weak voltage at both ends of a kernel of corn (Fig. 11.5). In fact, if you look carefully at various fruits such as apples, you will find positive and negative poles in each one.

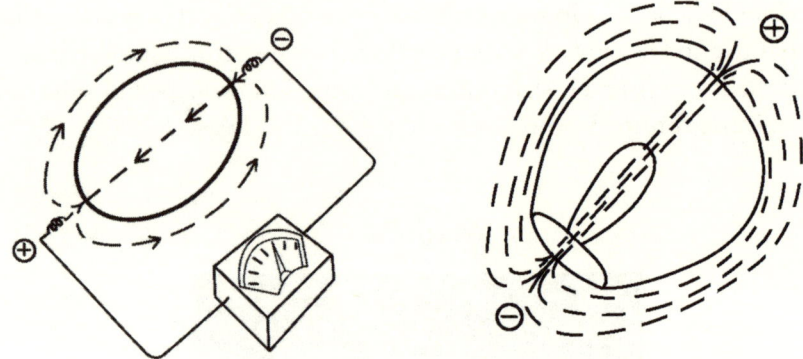

Figure 11.5 Magnetic Fields of an Egg and a Kernel of Corn

If you look at the shape of an apple, it appears that the energy of the apple is absorbed toward the stem of the apple. This energy then spreads out toward the opposite end of the apple (Fig. 11.6). This is the so-called "explosion" or "Big Bang" of an apple. The shape of an apple is determined by this energy, which aligns and arranges the substances that compose the apple.

Figure 11.6 Magnetic Field of an Apple

We can see the same energetic and structural configuration in the human body. A woman's uterus connects with the fallopian tubes that absorb the eggs and through its lower part called cervix, a birth of an infant will eventually take place (Fig. 11.7). The fallopian tubes and the cervix have a funnel-like shape, similar to the Black and White Holes. The only difference between the shape of a woman's reproductive system and that of the universe is that there are two fallopian tubes, while there is only one original Black Hole in the universe.

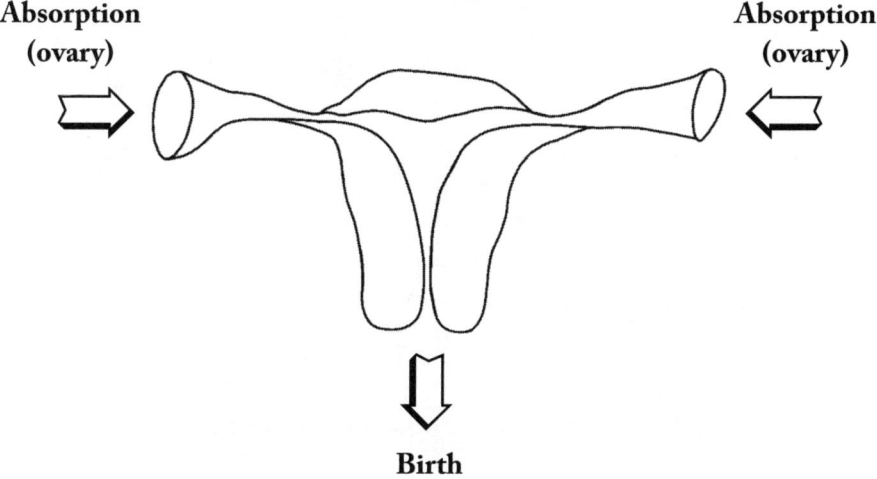

Figure 11.7 Black and White Holes of the Uterus

Human Energy Channels

Human beings have the same form and function as the universe. Cosmic energy (yang) is absorbed through the nose (air), while cosmic substance (yin) is absorbed through the mouth (food and drink). Cosmic energy and cosmic substances are transformed into the vital energy (Qi) required by the body. The yin actions of the body manifest as the body's excretions (urine, feces, semen, etc.). These substances are able to give nourishment to the planet and aid in the process of birth and renewal. The yang actions of the body manifest as Qi, which circulates in channels and nourishes the body and mind.

The body has six yin channels (or meridians, along which acupuncture points are located) and six yang channels. In addition, two special channels, the Ren, or "Conception" channel and the Du, or "Governing" channel, control the yin and yang of the body. Because the body reflects the orientation of the universe, the Ren and Du channels flow in the same direction as the flow of stars during a Big Bang. There is another special channel called the Chong, or "Penetrating" channel, which flows along the major axis of the human body. This channel is the same as the major axis of the universe (Fig. 11.8).

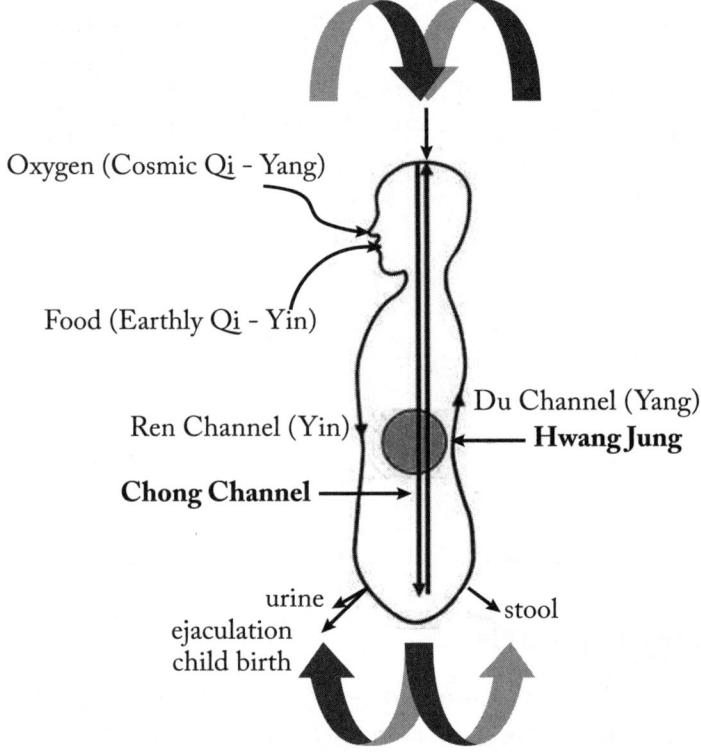

Figure 11.8 Human Energy Channels

In the center of the Chong channel is a mysterious place called *Hwang Jung*, literally translated as "the Golden Courtyard." This is believed to be the origin of life and death in a person. Human beings are programmed to flow from birth towards death. The *Hwang Jung* can actually change the direction of this flow. The birth of the universe began with the White Hole and its destruction will begin at the mouth of the Black Hole. The interface of the Black Hole and the White Hole is the *Hwang Jung*.

CHAPTER 12
Yin and Yang of Sleep

Currently there are over 40 million Americans suffering from some form of chronic sleep disorder. The suffering these people go through everyday of their lives is unspeakable. It is truly a national tragedy and an epidemic because sleeping is not only one of the greatest joys in life, but also one of the most important facets of our health. To live healthy, prosperous and long lives, we must be able to get a deep and sound sleep on a daily basis. On average we spend one-third of our lives in sleep. The ability to fall asleep quickly, sleep deeply, and wake up refreshed and recharged for the new day's activity is a vital indicator of the state of your health. If you are in generally good health, no matter how fatigued you are, you should be able to fully recover with a good night's sleep. Let's first discuss several factors that make up deep, sound sleep.

What is a Deep, Sound Sleep?

To begin, we should discuss insomnia. According to the *Merck Manual*, insomnia is a lack of sleep due to trouble falling or staying asleep or a disturbance in sleep patterns.[1] To further elaborate, insomnia is an inability to fall asleep within a half hour of lying down in bed, awakening more than five times during sleep, and having difficulty falling back to sleep within 30 minutes after awakening at night.

By contrast, if you fall asleep quickly, sleep deeply and fall back asleep quickly upon awakening, then your sleep habits are healthy. After a good night's sleep, you should be able to awake at a predetermined time and feel light and refreshed, ready for a brand new day. Additionally, sound sleep means having a sufficient rapid-eye-movement (REM) sleep. This is the phase of sleep where dreaming takes place. If there is a significant reduction in this REM sleep, no matter how much you sleep you will feel fatigued, lethargic and groggy. You will experience a heightened sensitivity to various stimuli around you, a decline in memory and concentration, and possibly even sexual dysfunction.

The benefits of deep, sound, restful, quality sleep are numerous: health, vitality, a strong immune system, clear thinking and sound memory, just to name a few.

The Natural Cycle of Sleep

When we observe nature, we can sense a certain rhythm or cycle at play. In the spring, we can see the sprouting (yang) of seeds and in the fall, the falling (yin) of leaves. In the sky we can see the waxing (yang) and waning (yin) of the moon and the rise (yang) and the setting (yin) of the sun. In the ocean we can see the flow (yang) and ebb (yin) of the tide. These are but a few examples of the natural rhythms or the dynamics of yin and yang in nature.

Human life also consists of a certain rhythm of activity (yang) and rest (yin). Like the natural cycles, these two activities must follow a certain rhythm. If the natural rhythm of activity and rest is disturbed the consequences can be serious, such as a breakdown in one's health–physically, mentally and emotionally.

Applying yin-yang theory in our daily lives is crucial because it is a relativistic, holistic and balanced way of thinking.

The Consequences of Breaking Natural Rhythm

Whenever we break our natural cycles, there are certain consequences that we must endure. If we missed a good night's sleep, for instance, we will be unable to function normally or work efficiently. We will be fatigued, moody and irritable, with a lack of focus and poor memory. We will be more prone to mistakes and accidents and susceptible to illnesses. In addition to these short-term side effects, there can also be long-term, serious consequences to our health when we go against our natural rhythms.

A few years ago there was a report on the relationship between sleep and colon cancer on a local TV news station.[2] According to the report, researchers found that nurses who worked night shifts had a significantly higher incidence of colon cancer than those who worked regular shifts. Another report by The

Associated Press (11-29-07) discussed several studies which showed increased risk of breast cancer in women and higher incidence of prostate cancer in men working at night for many years. The probable cause, according to the report, is due to the disruption in the body's normal (circadian) rhythm interfering with the normal production of melatonin, which fights against the cancer cells, and the disruption of the natural healing and regeneration processes such as cell division and DNA repair.

In the Yin-Yang of Physiology section (Chapter 2), we discussed the different types of hormones that are produced during the day and at night. In the daytime (yang), there is an increased production of cortisone and adrenaline, while at nighttime (yin), growth hormone and melatonin are produced. So if there is a disruption in this natural yin and yang cycle, the body will not function properly and will breakdown faster. Now let's try to further understand these facts according to the yin and yang principle.

Sleeping According to Nature

Sleeping according to nature is the same as sleeping according to a natural rhythm. Everybody has different circadian cycles but will generally follow the natural cycles of day and night. Some people go to bed early and wake up early, which is the most beneficial for a healthy body since this pattern is most aligned with the cycles of nature. Others thrive at night, saying they can work through the night without any problems, but this is not necessarily healthy for them in the long run.

Night is yin time and should be reserved for rest, recuperation and repair. Both your body and mind need deep rest in order to recharge so that you can wake up refreshed for an active life during the daytime. In the daytime it is yang energy that makes our life possible. Everything that you do from the very moment that you wake up to the end of the day just prior to falling asleep is controlled by yang energy.

Being active at night actually depletes yin energy. It is yin energy that holds or contains yang, and since the night is yin, it must hold yang (activity) within the body so that in the morning yang can go about its dynamic activity. Simply stated, the better yin contains yang during the night, the more restful sleep you will have and the fresher you will wake up the next morning. In contrast, the weaker the yin is in its ability to hold yang, the lighter and more disturbed the sleep will be with a lot of restless dreaming. Having plenty of yin in reserve will allow your mind and spirit to rest peacefully at night.

Another factor to consider is the amount of yang energy burnt at night in relation to the day time. It is believed in eastern medicine that working at night actually depletes yang at least twice as much as comparable work during the day. Thus, in addition to depleting yin energy, you are also rapidly burning yang energy. All of us have finite yin and yang energies and so if you burn them at a faster pace, you will accelerate the aging process and weaken your health.

We can discuss the consequence of burning both yin and yang energies in terms of western science. Science tells us that the best time to sleep is between 10:00 pm to 3:00 am. Why? It is because your body's old, damaged and dead cells are actively being replaced with new cells. Thus at this time, any activity, whether physical or mental, will divert the energy from that exchange and hinder the natural healing process. In simple terms, you will simply age and deteriorate faster if you do not sleep between these hours.

The bottom line is the more you break the rules of nature, the more damage you will inflict on your body and mind. On the other hand, by following the laws of nature, you will naturally live longer, healthier and happier and have an overall balanced life.

The Main Cause of Insomnia

Though there are many causes of insomnia, such as over stimulation (TV, radio, Internet), environmental noise, aches and pains due to illness, stimulant drugs, etc., the most direct cause of insomnia is the brain's over-activity and the resulting blood congestion in the head. During the day, which is a time of activity, the blood is supplied mainly to the arms and legs, as well as to the head so that one can stay awake and physical and mental activities can take place. When night time comes, the blood supply to those actively functioning areas is substantially reduced and instead is stored in the internal organs. Thus, only the absolute amount necessary for survival is sent to those areas so that the arms and legs feel tired and want to rest, while the head feels empty and sleepy.

If, however, the blood gets congested in the head instead of being gathered and stored in the internal organs due to various reasons, there will be insomnia. Thus the chief, direct cause of insomnia is the congestion of blood in the head and the solution is to simply bring the blood down from the head.

If the average person has trouble falling asleep, he or she will toss and turn about. This brings about an obsession with falling asleep, which will further increase blood congestion in the head and make falling asleep much more difficult. To decongest the blood away from the brain, it is better to sit rather than lie down, and even better to stand.

The Hot Head, Cold Feet Syndrome

Eastern medicine advises people that they should keep their feet warm and heads cool. We've all heard the expression, "Keep your cool!" For your sleep, health and relationship with others, this is sound advice. When the head is kept cool and the feet warm, normal blood circulation takes place. But for most people living in the city, they literally have cold feet and hot heads. This is the "hot head" syndrome or "getting fired up." The head is literally "on fire" due to agitation and the blood congestion in the head increases. You just will not be able to fall asleep in this state.

Fire (yang) by nature likes to rise while water (yin) descends. If the fire is only at the top and the water at the bottom, what will happen is that by nature they will separate. In terms of your life, death occurs when the fire and water go their own ways. By contrast, when the fire and water interact, exchange and communicate with each other, there is life, health and longevity. Thus eastern medicine says that when there is a cool head and warm feet, you will not only have deep, sound sleep, but you will also not get sick!

The Sleeping Pattern: In Tune with Seasons

To achieve longevity eastern medicine recommends that one's sleep pattern should change with the seasons. It advises us that since everything is beginning to spring forth (rising of yang energy) in the springtime, one should get to bed early (to conserve yang energy) and wake up early (to activate the yang). Because summer time is the most yang time of the year, there is exuberant activity and growth (spreading and dispersing of yang). So one should be active as much as possible and extend the time of activity (that is why we have summer time). One should get to bed late (but not past midnight) and then wake up as early as possible. Autumn is the time of gathering, harvesting and slowing down. One should get to bed early and rise early like the spring time. Here one should facilitate the gathering of yang energy by sleeping early and then waking up early to most efficiently utilize yang during the day. In the winter time, one needs to conserve as much yang energy as possible since it is the time of rest and hibernation (yin). Therefore, one needs to get to bed early and then rise late.

To recap:

- ❖ spring: early to bed, early to rise
- ❖ summer: late to bed, early to rise
- ❖ autumn: early to bed, early to rise
- ❖ winter: early to bed, late to rise

How Many Hours Should You Sleep?

This all depends on the physical and mental types of work you do. In general experts recommend between six to eight hours of sleep. Some people do fine with five to six hours of sleep while others need nine or more hours. But six to eight hours is average. The number of hours is very important, but the quality of sleep is even more important.

The elderly generally need less sleep. Why? Sleeping time is related to growth. Growth hormone is produced at night when one is sleeping. That is why babies sleep so much. As they are very yang in nature, they need a lot of sleep (yin) to balance their dynamic yang. Elders meanwhile, need less sleep because they do not need to grow.

Beds, Pillows and Room Temperature

The selection of the proper mattress is intimately related to sound sleep. Though there will be personal preferences, it is best to sleep on a mattress that is not too hard or soft. On the average, we move about 20 times during the night. This is the body's natural process to help our blood circulation. So we must not impede this process by sleeping on overly hard or soft beds.

The main factor in mattress selection is its comfort level. This will depend on how firm a mattress can evenly support every part of the body. You should also consider your height, weight and body structure. Another factor to consider is certain disease conditions such as low back pain, arthritis or neuralgia, where a firmer mattress can prevent excessive bodily movements so that healing can better take place. Additional factors include the mattress's heat-retention ability and the proper absorption of sweat.[3]

In terms of pillows, there is an eastern saying that goes, "The higher the pillow, the shorter the life span." So it is better not to use high pillows unless you have medical conditions such as acid reflux, asthma, or the common cold or flu where you are having difficulty breathing when lying down flat. Use a pillow that will allow free bodily movements. For softer mattresses, use lower pillows and with firmer mattresses, slightly higher pillows.

Not only are the mattress and the pillow important, but equally important is the temperature of the room. This will vary from person to person, since those who have a lot of heat in their bodies (yang) will obviously want their rooms cool with air-conditioning running all night, while others with cold bodies (yin) abhor the very idea of it. In general, 18-20° Celcius (64.4° F - 68° F) is appropriate for sleeping with 40 to 50 percent humidity. If the room is over 24° C (75.2° F) degrees, you cannot have a deep sleep. For children (who are more yang and thus have more heat) 18° C (64.4° F) is the best.[4]

Regardless of mattresses, pillows or room temperature, you should be able to fall asleep quickly and "sleep like a log," if you are in balanced health.

Sleep Position

Buddha is said to have slept on his right side. Anatomically speaking, this is in alignment with the pathway of your digestive system. The amount of oxygen and blood that circulates into the lungs is greater if you are lying on the right side in comparison to the left. Also by sleeping on the right side, you can avoid listening to the heart beat, which can at times keep you awake. Thus, the best natural position is with both of your knees bent, and the left leg naturally on the top of right.

In terms of yin-yang, eastern medicine considers the right side of the body as yang. This is because for most people, the right hand is stronger, faster, freer or less restricted in movement. Heaven is considered yang, while the earth is considered yin. Thus, by placing the right side (yang) of your body to the ground/bed (yin) there is a natural balance of yin and yang, thereby inducing better sleep.

Ways to Fall Asleep Quickly and Sleep Deeply

Sleep is considered yin in relation to an awakened, conscious state. So by putting yourself into a yin or relaxed/calm state, sleep will come about naturally. In order to achieve this, the first and foremost recommendation in eastern medicine is meditation.

(1) Meditation

When you have trouble falling asleep, sit calmly in a cross-legged position and focus your mind on the *Dantian*, which is translated literally as "Elixir Field" and is located approximately three inches below the navel. This is your center of gravity. Your breathing will gradually become deeper, longer and regular, and within 30 minutes you should be able to fall asleep. If not, then just continue to sit quietly in this position and you will eventually fall asleep. This is the most natural form of breathing meditation and when done properly, it will increase your energy in a much shorter amount of time than in sleep. You will thus need less sleep. Many masters and sages of the East are said to have replaced their normal eight hours of sleep with less than one hour of deep meditation.

For most people, quietly focusing on *Dantian* will help them fall asleep. If you still cannot sleep, just continue until you do fall asleep even if it takes several hours. If you continue to become anxious by thinking whether or not this method is working or why it's taking so long to fall asleep, or if you worry about what to do the next day, then your brain's activity will increase and so will the blood congestion in your head. Remember that we are simply trying to bring our awareness to the lower abdomen and not to the head.

Just relax your shoulders and drop them down and bring up an image of the time when you were most relaxed and comfortable. Then focus on your lower abdomen. You will fall asleep. Remember that the stronger your thoughts about falling asleep, the more trouble you will have falling asleep. This is similar to when things do not turn out well if you become excessively greedy.

Another way to disperse the blood congestion in the head or brain is to stand in what is known as "horse stance." This is the most famous of all martial arts stances and has similar effects as the cross-legged sitting. However, it is more effective in pulling down the congested blood in the head. The reason for this is that the energy becomes strongly concentrated in the legs when you are standing, and this will quickly disperse the blood congestion in the head.

Open your feet and legs to your shoulders' width or slightly wider and keep your body in an upright position. Now bend your knees so that you can barely see the tips of your toes. Your arms should be in a position as if holding the reins of horses. You are actually mimicking the horse riding position. Try to release all tension from the body. If you can maintain this position for a few minutes, you will feel slightly fatigued, which will help you fall asleep.

The two methods above are excellent for fundamentally correcting the energy imbalance in the body. They will help bring the blood down from the head. Remember that in eastern medicine, most illnesses are due to the inability of energy to descend. The *Dantian* is the warehouse of energy in the body and so it must be sufficiently charged with energy. But if the energy that should be in the *Dantian* is dispersed to other areas of body, many illnesses can result. Similar to the "hot head, cold feet syndrome" previously mentioned, a combination of an emptiness of energy in the *Dantian* and a fullness of energy in the head results in insomnia.

Another simple exercise to help you achieve deeper, sounder sleep is to focus your attention on inhaling air down to your *Dantian*. Then exhale the air down to the center of your soles. Repeat this exercise until you fall asleep.

If you consistently practice these three methods of meditation, not only will your insomnia improve, but so will the health of your whole body.

(2) Additional Suggestions

1. Light Exercise: Try to stretch and breathe deeply for a few minutes before you get in bed. Movements from Yoga, Qigong, or Tai Chi are excellent. Avoid, however, any rigorous physical exercise at least two to three hours prior to sleeping because you can be overly stimulated. Taking a walk for 30 to 40 minutes after dinner can help you sleep better.

2. Try to eliminate mental tension by changing your thought pattern and attitude towards life:

- Relax and stop worrying! Experts state that most of the things people worry about never happen. In fact, 98% of all worries are never realized. So why waste time, energy and valuable sleep thinking about your worries.
- Forgive and forget! Let it go and move on with life.
- Have sincere gratitude! Just be thankful for everything you have now.

Again, you can practice Yoga and other meditations to help reduce mental tension. Jotting down or journaling your worries and concerns can also help you see things more objectively and help you take better action toward them. A light massage, a hot bath or a shower are also very good. Just soaking your feet in hot water will help.

3. Those who are suffering from insomnia generally hold a lot of tension in their necks and upper shoulders. Relaxing them will help the process of sleep. So try to develop a daily habit of stretching your neck and shoulders, preferably several times throughout the day and especially just before your bedtime. You can also perform a tension-relaxation exercise in which you alternately tense and relax your muscles from head to toe while lying down.

4. Try not to eat right before going to sleep because eating will keep your brain active. A maxim of the East states that, "If you eat and go to sleep, you lose one day of your life," and, "If you drink and go to sleep you lose one month of your life." The liver is busy detoxifying your system at night so if you put food—or even worse, alcohol—into your system, the process of detoxification is hindered. Thus you will obviously age faster.

5. Try to limit or avoid taking any forms of stimulants such as coffee, tea or carbonated beverages with caffeine. Many diet supplements, appetite suppressants, and decongestants in cough medicine can over stimulate your system, so try to avoid these as well.

6. Limit TV, radio, and the Internet before bedtime.

7. Whatever you do to help you fall asleep, try not to fight the sleep– instead you need to surrender and just let it happen. Release your fear about insomnia. The shortcut to falling and having a deep, sound sleep is to accept

even the insomnia itself. If you cannot fall asleep after lying in bed for 20 to 30 minutes, go to another room and perform some light activity. You can read books of inspiration and hope, or self-improvement books. But don't do any heavy reading. You can also try to listen to soft, classical music or meditation music. Avoid heavy rock music.

8. One of the most important facets of health is regularity. Not only should you eat at regularly scheduled mealtimes, but you should also keep regular sleep hours. It facilitates falling asleep quickly.

9. For a sound sleep, keep the room as dark as possible and keep the noise out. Using a "white noise" machine can help block outside noise.

10. Sleep experts recommend getting 30 to 40 minutes of sunlight in the morning hours because it can better regulate body's natural biological clock. This in turn will induce better sleep at night as well as improve overall health.

11. Try to avoid taking naps after 3:00 pm and limit the duration of naps to under 30 minutes.

12. According to color therapy, violet helps induce sleep. By darkening the room and imagining the color in your mind, you can bring on peaceful sleep. Violet is associated with the crown chakra and is considered to be a color of meditation and enlightenment.

13. Eat walnut porridge - For thousands of years in the East, walnuts have been used for insomnia. Walnuts relieve fatigue and boost both physical and mental energy. If you observe a walnut carefully, it resembles a brain (Doctrine of Signatures). Walnuts are delicious and can be eaten on a daily basis.

14. Apples, which are yin in nature, also have an effect on inducing sound sleep. Take the core or seed region out of an apple, add one tablespoon of honey and steam it. Drink the juice about one hour before bedtime.

15. Drink a vegetable juice composed of celery and lettuce, both of which are yin vegetables that have a sleep-inducing effect. Adding crown daisy will enhance this effect.

16. An eastern herb called rehmannia root is quite effective for calming the mind. Taking this herb (8-12 grams) boiled in half a liter of water and di-

vided in several doses throughout the day is effective. Rehmannia is a famous blood tonic and one of the most yin-natured herbs. Going back to yin-yang theory, night time is yin and your body and mind need yin to calm their yang, active part.

17. Other eastern herbs commonly used for insomnia include:

- Wild jujube: calms the mind and gathers energy inward; nourishes the Heart and the Liver; good for people who are stressed, anxious and easily frightened.
- Biota seed: good for people who are very sensitive, restless and suffer from constipation.
- Morus fruit: nurtures blood; treats anemia, high blood pressure, constipation, and neurasthenia.
- Longan fruit: nurtures blood and calms the Heart; treats forgetfulness, excessive dreaming and palpitations.
- Lotus seed: an astringent herb commonly used for diarrhea, seminal emission, high blood pressure and palpitations.
- Bamboo shavings: treats anxiety, restlessness, tension, depression, and excessive tension in the head and face.
- Juncus: this is a pith of common rush and can strongly calm the mind. It is also used as a diuretic.

18. If nothing else works, try not to go to sleep. Again, don't fight it. Your body will eventually fall asleep as needed. Finally, in the words of a popular Zen saying, "Eat when you are hungry; sleep when you are sleepy."

CHAPTER 13

Yin and Yang of Performance Enhancing Drugs: Is Too Much Sex Bad for You?

The manufacturers of the top three performance enhancing drugs (PEDs), Viagra (sildenafil citrate), Levitra (vardenafil) and Cialis (tadalafil) spent an estimated $400 to $500 million dollars in the year 2004 trying to convince men, and women, that the solution to impotency comes in a pill. In a free market advertising is fundamental to any successful business. But by definition product advertisements do not tell the whole story, or at least they do not give equal weight to the benefits and dangers of what they are trying to sell. While ads boldly tout the effectiveness and advantages of performance enhancing drugs, warnings of potential side effects are squeezed into hurried disclaimers.

In a recent interview, 57-year-old actor James Woods joked that he was "surprised [he] didn't die of a heart attack" while having more than six-and-a-half hours of Viagra-maintained sex. While Wood's comment was most likely made in jest, it raises important concerns about the potential dangers of PEDs.

In this chapter we will explore how performance enhancing drugs work and why they have become so popular, and we will take a look at the consequences of their increased popularity. We will also offer a holistic interpretation of the drugs and their effects on the body.

Causes of Erectile Dysfunction (Impotence)

Erectile Dysfunction (ED), commonly known as impotence, is the inability of the male to initiate and maintain penile erection. Studies estimate that about

30 million men in the United States and 152 million men worldwide, or about one half of all men over the age of 40, suffer from varying degrees of ED. Although there are psychological causes for ED (stress, depression, performance anxiety), the primary cause in 90 percent of men over 40 is physical. Most common are problems with blood vessels due to atherosclerosis (hypertension), high cholesterol, blood clots or surgery, and problems associated with neurological disorders caused by diabetes, multiple sclerosis, stroke, injury, alcoholism or drugs. In addition, ED may be caused by smoking, hormonal imbalance, and physical abnormalities of the penis. Because ED's root causes are often physical, doctors are beginning to recognize that ED can be an early sign of other, more serious, conditions.

How Performance Enhancing Drugs Work

When a man is physically healthy, his body generates and, when sexually stimulated, releases sufficient amounts of the chemical nitric oxide (NO) to produce an erection. In physically unhealthy men, the production or release of NO can be retarded, preventing or inhibiting a sustained erection. In this case, ED is the sign of a more serious condition.

Following ejaculation, certain substances work to temper the effect of NO, extinguishing the erection for a period of time. This is a protective mechanism to give the body time to recuperate and manufacture more sperm. Contrary to popular opinion, this is the way the body is intended to work. When the body is weak, it protects itself from physical strain that may cause greater damage to an already taxed system.

Performance enhancing drugs, such as Viagra, Levitra and Cialis, enhance the effect of NO. They prevent the extinguishing of the erection after ejaculation and they allow men with health problems to maintain erections when they are otherwise unable.

Problems with Performance Enhancing Drugs

In healthy men PEDs cancel the necessary downtime between erections, and in unhealthy men drugs allow for sexual activity when the body is cautioning against it. Moreover, because these drugs are manufactured as part of a symptomatic approach to health care—addressing symptoms rather than causes—they work regardless of a man's age, health or cause of sexual dysfunction; they override the body's natural protective mechanisms. Performance enhancing drugs work independently of the other systems of the body. They ignore the good of the whole for the sake of instant gratification.

And then there are the side effects.

Side Effects

Common side effects of performance enhancing drugs are headaches, facial flushing, indigestion, diarrhea, muscle aches, nasal stuffiness and vision problems. Less frequent side effects include asthma, seizures and low blood pressure. In men with pre-existing heart conditions these drugs have been known to cause heart attacks, strokes, high blood pressure and even sudden death.

While the number, variety and potential severity of side effects should be enough to give one pause, there is another aspect of health that should be considered.

The Energy of Sex

Sex drains a man's energy. Research on the effects of sex on athletic performance indicates that in men sexual activity, particularly with ejaculation, diminishes overall energy. (Conversely, women appear to have more energy after intercourse.) Furthermore, the general consensus of the medical community is that sexual activity strains the heart as much as many forms of exercise and must be limited in those suffering from heart conditions.

Given the strain that sex puts on the body, one must ask whether men with ED are healthy enough to engage in such activity, particularly when it uses up energy needed to maintain the functioning of other bodily systems.

An Eastern (Holistic) Medical Perspective

The performance enhancing drug, a symptomatic approach to "curing" ED, dismisses the body's natural safety mechanisms, mechanisms naturally designed to prevent further weakening of more essential bodily systems. Taking performance enhancing drugs allows men to engage in sexual activity regardless of their overall state of health. This can be a dangerous unbalancing act.

Eastern medicine seeks to establish balance, and thereby health, in a system that is out of alignment. It does this by reestablishing order to two opposing forces called yin and yang. Remember that yin and yang are more than a fixed pair of complementary opposites; they are also dynamic forces that are constantly changing and balancing in relation to one another. When we look at our health in this light, we see that the state of the human body is a dynamic equilibrium. It is a unit of opposing forces that define, refine and balance one another.

Eastern medicine speaks of the yin-yang perspective, which simply states that every situation must be looked at in terms of its benefit (yang) and harm (yin), or the positive (yang) and negative (yin) impact it may have. We must look at the whole (yang) as well as the parts (yin), the present (yang) and the future (yin), and long term consequences (yin) as opposed to immediate gratification (yang). Both perspectives are essential. One cannot exist without the other. Looking at the total picture is what the holistic view is about.

Performance Enhancing Drugs in a Different Light

As previously mentioned, performance enhancing drugs are designed to meet a specific, one-time objective. The overall health of the bodily system and the underlying cause of the dysfunction are considered non-issues for their purposes. Applying the principles of yin and yang, however, we evaluate whether the risks to general health outweigh the benefits and if the short-term results outweigh the long-term consequences.

A man who is impotent due to underlying weakness will become more depleted with repeated erections and ejaculations. The energy being used for sex is being pulled from other more essential systems. This is like going on a shopping spree with money budgeted for food. Just as priorities must be set in terms of financial responsibility, the body also needs to prioritize its utilization of available substance and energy. This depletion of the body's resources may surface as weakened immunity, depression, fatigue, the worsening of pre-existing health problems or, in extreme cases, death. In addition, abuse of performance enhancing drugs leads to low quality sperm. A child spawned with the aid of performance enhancing drugs is more likely to have health problems than one who is not.

For the same reason, the use of Viagra may also increase the probability of birth defects. According to the *Merck Manual*, the risk of birth defects increases for parents over 50.[1] In other words, there is a greater risk of birth defects as the age of the men increases.

Neglecting health issues that create impotence and using a symptomatic approach to treat the problem may be simple and convenient, but in the long term it is counterproductive at best and dangerous at worst. The underlying causes of impotence may be significant health risks that must be diagnosed and treated, otherwise the havoc that they can create in the body may go unnoticed until it is too late.

How Eastern Medicine Diagnoses and Treats Erectile Dysfunction

Let us first discuss the concept of the "Three Treasures" which are Jing, Qi and Shen, translated as essence, energy and spirit. These are intimately related to sexual health and performance.

1. Imbalance of Qi (Vital Energy):

All illnesses, including ED, have their root in the imbalance of Qi. Thus, when we fall ill we either have too much or too little Qi, it is either blocked or there is chaotic circulation of Qi. Only when there is balance and harmony in the quantity, speed, time and direction of Qi, can our healing system properly kick-in and optimally heal the problem. In general, there is a lack of yang Qi or *Source Qi* in ED. The *Source Qi* is the active or yang aspect of the essence known as Jing.

2. Lack of Jing (Essence):

Jing is the Essence needed for sexual activity as well as overall health and longevity–learning how to preserve, increase and strengthen the Essence will help improve sexual prowess. According to eastern medicine Jing is stored in the Kidneys and governs the birth, growth and development of our entire being. Since we are born with a fixed amount of Jing, it is gradually depleted or consumed over our lifetime. The very process of aging indicates the weakening of this Jing. So the faster we consume it, i.e. overworking, excessive sexual activity, poor nutrition, etc., the shorter our lifespan.

3. Imbalance of Shen (Spirit):

In eastern medicine, the various emotions are under the control of our Shen, which is stored in our Heart. If our emotions go overboard, they can greatly harm our Shen or the Heart. So with continued emotional disturbances such as anger, fear, fright, worry and anxiety over a period of time, our Hearts will be out of balance. In eastern medicine, the Heart and Kidneys share an intimate relationship. Any disturbance to the Heart, therefore, will directly impact the Kidneys, the organ of sex. The emotions of fear and fright in particular are directly related to the Kidneys and so will cause significant damage to them over time. This will result in ED. Fear and fright descend the energy and thus hinder the ascending or rising energy needed for sexual arousal. It is a well-known fact that if someone is suddenly frightened, they can lose control of their urination or bowel function.

Although there are other causes of ED in eastern medicine, such as physical trauma, all of them more or less fall into one of the above three categories of imbalance. Therefore, to properly treat ED, all three areas must be addressed.

How to Build the Three Treasures

There are three main ways to build the Three Treasures. First is through spiritual cultivation using breathing and meditation. This is absorbing the so-called "heavenly energy." The next is through proper foods and supplements. This is the "earthly energy."

The third way is through the actual sexual practice itself. This last method was briefly discussed in Chapter 3 (Yin and Yang of Sex). Here, we will elaborate on the first two ways to boost sexual energy. Remember, however, that there are no quick fixes, and that the health of the entire body must be considered. Only then will we be able to possess radiant sexual energy.

Breathing, Meditation and Exercises

1. Meditation: practice the standing and sitting meditation exercises as described in the previous chapter (Ch. 12: Yin and Yang of Sleep). A simple breathing technique that you can add is to first exhale completely through the mouth to eliminate stale air and then slowly breathe in through the nose to the count of four, then hold your breath for two and finally exhale slowly through the nose

for four. Try to keep the tip of your tongue touching the roof of your mouth (upper palate) throughout the breathing cycle. Repeat this breathing exercise for a specified time. Remember that meditation will effectively help build and conserve *Source Qi*, the energy involved in sex.

It may seem that a strong sexual energy arises when there is wild excitement and commotion, which are yang states. But according to the principle of yin and yang, extreme yang always converts to yin. So like a candle with a short fuse, the fire lasts only for a short time. In reality, a strong passionate energy that is sustaining arises when one is calm, relaxed, and in a peaceful, meditative state. It is from this yin state that a strong yang or fire can spring forth.

2. Get all your emotions under control. We discussed how the emotions of fear and fright descend energy and weaken sexual energy. Here we need to discuss the importance of controlling anger. The arousal of sexual energy is closely related to the emotion of anger because of its yang nature. While a slight amount of anger can activate the body's sexual energy, an extreme or prolonged anger will actually weaken or damage it because the energy of anger rises upward (yang) and leaves no energy "downstairs" for the reproductive system. The so-called "hot-head syndrome" as mentioned in the last chapter applies here as well. This is the state of "excess above (head) and deficiency below (reproductive system)." Thus, anyone who has a lot of anger most likely has a weakened libido. The principle of extreme yang converting into yin applies here as well.

3. Kegel exercise: tightening and squeezing the pubococcygeus, or PC, muscles at least 100 times per day is recommended. (The PC muscles are the ones which help stop and start the flow of urine; for men Kegels may also include the cremaster muscle, which raise and lower the testicles.) You should also be tightening your rectum or anal sphincter. According to eastern medicine, exercising the PC and sphincter muscles has more than just physical benefits. The body has two major conduits of energy running along its front and the back called the Conception and the Governing channels, respectively (see Chapter 11: Yin and Yang of Universe for the diagram). When we tighten our PC and sphincter muscles and touch our tongue to the upper palate as recommended in Taoist meditation and qigong, we are creating what is known as a "Microcosmic Orbit." This is the connecting of the Conception and Governing

channels, both of which begin at the perineal region. This is the initial stage toward health and enlightenment. We are also activating what Yoga describes as the "Kundalini energy" from the base of our spine. This has a direct impact on our sexual energy, as well as, our overall health. Therefore, it is always good to keep our mouth and anal sphincter muscles "shut."

4. Massage: use your fingers to directly massage the perineal region, the K-1 acupuncture point located on the soles of the feet approximately one-third of the way from the base of second toe to the heel, and the DU-20 acupuncture point located at the apex of the head. Massage each area for 30 seconds to one minute using a clockwise circular motion.

5. Weight training: studies have shown that physical exercises, especially heavy weight training exercises that work the major muscle groups of the low back and lower body (both yin regions) such as squats, deadlifts and leg presses increased anti-aging hormones and testosterone levels in subjects. From an eastern medical perspective, these hormones are intimately related to the Kidneys, which govern the entire endocrine system. We can further understand how these exercises work by observing the relationship between the low back, legs and Kidneys.

6. In eastern medicine, the low back is considered to be the storehouse or the domain of the Kidneys. Thus exercising the low back will strengthen the Kidneys and improve sexual energy. For the same reason, it is also good to massage the low back as well. Sit down and rub both hands together until they are hot. Using brisk up and down motions, rub the low back for 30 seconds. Also exercise the entire lower body with brisk walking, hiking, bicycling, etc., since the lower body, too, is under the control of the Kidneys. The condition of your legs demonstrates the health of the whole body. You are only as old as your legs are. This applies to sexual energy as well, so always keep your legs healthy.

7. Try to maintain healthy body weight and eliminate potbellies. Not only are potbellies (extra fat stored around the abdomen) not generally considered sexy in our culture, but the sexual stamina of those who have them is usually suspect. Obesity also increases the likelihood of developing diabetes, high cholesterol levels and hypertension, which are some of the main causes of ED. Exercising the abdominal muscles will not only strengthen the internal organs

but will also boost sexual energy. Many acupuncture energy channels pass through the abdominal region and a place called the *Dantian* (Elixir Field), which as mentioned in chapter 12 is located in the lower abdomen approximately three inches below the belly button. The *Dantian* is the pivotal energy center that holds the Jing or Essence. This center is strengthened through abdominal exercises, which will help increase sexual energy.

By practicing these exercises on a regular basis, not only will your sexual energy be stronger, but your overall health will improve as well.

Foods and Supplements

A well-balanced diet is a must for increasing or maintaining sexual energy. Let's discuss various foods that were traditionally used as aphrodisiacs and how they work. Since the Kidneys contain both yin and yang elements, foods that contain the yang are able to strengthen sexual vitality, as will yin foods when appropriately combined with spices and/or wine. In terms of yin and yang, those substances from animals are the most yang, while those from vegetable and fruit sources are less yang.

Animal Sources:

• As mentioned in the Chapter 5 (Yin and Yang of Food and Diet), yin foods such as pork, oysters, sea cucumbers, duck and tortoise supply nutrients to the reproductive organs. When cooked with spices that act as aphrodisiacs themselves, and combined with white wine, these foods will quickly activate the body's sexual energy.

• Among the yin foods mentioned above, oysters happened to be one of the favorite foods of the legendary lover Casanova. Their dark color and primitive nature make them very yin. They supply fuel to the sexual organs.

• Shrimps have strong yang energy and are said to boost sexual energy. Shrimps have a tremendous reproductive capacity, producing thousands of eggs in a single sexual encounter. In the East, women whose husbands often travel for business are jokingly advised not to serve their husbands shrimps prior to their departure.

• Roe or fish eggs are known to boost sexual energy. All eggs have a balance of yin and yang and their energy goes to the reproductive system. Among the roe, the one with the greatest sexual energy-boosting effect is caviar.

• Loach (mudfish) is a very famous Asian dish, and a well known aphrodisiac. Though all fish are yin in nature, the very dynamic of loach, that of penetrating through lake bottoms or riverbeds, is very yang in nature and so can activate sexual energy. It is said that one can see the resurgence of sexual energy after only one week of regularly eating loach. It is a tremendous Kidney yang tonic. Snakes and eels also are dark colored, creepy animals, and so possess a yin nature. They are also animals that dig holes to live in, implying their strong penetrating action. For these reasons, all three animals are yang within yin, and so invigorate the yang energy within the Kidneys. Scientifically speaking, these animals will most likely encourage production of adrenal cortex hormones such as testosterone.

• Snakes, eels, and loaches are good for those who derive long lasting pleasure during sex, but have a problem initially feeling the urge for sex. It is better to eat these foods together with strong liquor, which will act as gunpowder, dynamically activating the yang energy.

• Mussels are another strong yang tonic famous for their effect on impotence and chronic low back pain, two of the cardinal symptoms of weakness in the Kidneys. They are said to raise overall body temperature but in particular that of the sexual organs. They can also benefit sexual dysfunction or nonresponsiveness in women.

• According to the Doctrine of Signatures, like treats the like. Thus, eating the organs of animals will strengthen the corresponding organs in the human body. Ingesting the kidneys of animals such as lamb, cow, pig and chicken will strengthen our kidneys and help strengthen our sexual energy. For the same reason, the male genitals of animals are eaten throughout various cultures, including cows, seals and deer.

• There is a saying in the East, "Men should not eat chicken wings." Chicken is a strong yang tonic and the wings are obviously a very yang part of the chicken. Thus chicken wings are considered a strong aphrodisiac and men who eat them may become overly amorous. A whole chicken is commonly cooked with ginseng in the East to help people quickly recover from various illnesses.

YIN AND YANG OF PERFORMANCE ENHANCING DRUGS

Plant Sources:

• All beans affect Kidneys as they are shaped in the form of Kidneys (Doctrine of Signatures), but black beans in particular have the strongest effect.

• Foods that are dark in color boost sexual performance because their energy is directed to the Kidneys. Black sesame seeds, dark chocolates and black soybeans are some of the foods that can enliven sexual energy.

• Seeds, similar to eggs, correspond to the Jing or Essence of the Kidneys and thus can boost sexual energy. In the East, sesame seeds are considered a super aphrodisiac and it is said that their regular ingestion over a long time will allow a person to overtake a running horse.

• Pumpkin seeds contain zinc and essential fatty acids, which are crucial in the formation of sperm.

• Walnuts are a famous yang tonic in eastern medicine. Again the Doctrine of Signatures applies here as the shape of walnuts resembles the kidneys, lungs and brain, and all three of these organs are strengthened by eating them.

• Peaches are one of the more yang fruits that can help sexual energy. Cleopatra is said to have enjoyed eating them.

• Truffles are a fungus/mushroom that were savored by Napoleon Bonaparte, a military leader notorious in his quest for power, and the French writer-doctor François Rabelais, who shocked polite society with his sometimes bawdy tales. It is said that one should not eat them if one wants to maintain calm and chastity.

• Cocoa powder is derived from the cacao seed and was the favorite drink of Montezuma II, emperor of the Aztecs in the early 16th century, famous for his many mistresses. He is known to have had no fewer than 50 portions of it daily. Recent research demonstrated that cocoa and dark chocolate may lower blood pressure and keep the heart healthy. The flavonol found in cocoa actually helps the body utilize nitric oxide, which as previously mentioned is the chemical responsible for widening the arteries and is necessary for attaining and maintaining an erection.

• Vanilla is commonly known in the West as an aphrodisiac. It has been shown to increase the levels of adrenaline, which boosts the supply of oxygen and glucose to the brain and muscles during danger or excitement. Vanilla beans are very dark brown (yin) in color with a remarkably strong aromatic fragrance (yang). Thus, vanilla can strengthen both the yin and the yang of the Kidneys. It was traditionally used to season the famous chocolate beverage of the Aztecs.

• Saw Palmetto, a fruit native to North America, was traditionally consumed as a food by the American Indians as well as a treatment for various urinary and reproductive conditions. It is now a famous herb in the treatment of enlarged prostate in men. It is also used for impotence, premature ejaculation and decreased libido. It is especially useful in what is known as "psychic" impotence, or impotence caused by psychological factors.

• Garlic is also very good for sexual vitality. Try eating garlic with meat for one week and compare the effects to that of Viagra. You may find that they stimulate your sexual impulses in a longer and more continued way than Viagra. For these reasons, garlic is one of the forbidden foods for Buddhist monks living in the temple so as not to interfere with their spiritual training. By eating plenty of garlic, men's erections in the morning will be better, and women who pass by these men will look more beautiful to them. In fact, whether or not women around you look more attractive than ordinary times is a yardstick you can use yourself to measure your own sexual vitality.

• Onions were considered a tonic by the ancient Egyptians. They are known to prevent and treat hypertension, atherosclerosis and augment the kidneys' functioning. Though not as potent an aphrodisiac as garlic, onions can nonetheless increase sexual energy.

• **Five Forbidden Foods:** traditionally, there were five foods that the Buddhist and Taoist monks were forbidden to eat. These foods are known to increase sexual desires and so were shunned by people who were purifying and cultivating themselves spiritually. As mentioned previously, engaging in excessive sexual activity can deplete the Jing or Essence and impede the goal of achieving enlightenment. The five forbidden foods in the Buddhist tradition are wild rocambole and squill (both are plants similar to onions), green onion, garlic and chives. The foods in the Taoist tradition are leeks, purple onion, garlic, rape (weed) and squill.

YIN AND YANG OF PERFORMANCE ENHANCING DRUGS

In addition to the common foods mentioned above, there are many unusual, even bizarre, substances that have traditionally been used as aphrodisiacs in various cultures around the world. Just to name a few, the list includes semen, menstrual blood, animal parts, toad's venom, musk and a toxic beetle known as Spanish fly.

We will next discuss famous herbal remedies for treating male impotence. Here again, there are many wild claims regarding the boosting of sexual energy, but we will discuss only the ones that are commonly used in eastern medicine.

In the eastern pharmacopeia, a few herbs in the qi tonic category and all herbs in the yang tonic category help boost sexual energy. The two most famous of these herbs are deer horn and ginseng.

Deer horn: among animals, deer are the most yang in nature, their yang energy being easily activated and set in motion. Thus, they are highly sensitive and easily frightened. The yang energy ascends and penetrates the head to create their horns. The head is the most yang part of the body. And the most yang of this part is the velvet that springs forth in the springtime. This is the reason why the deer horn is considered the number one aphrodisiac in eastern medicine. But it is also considered the number one general tonic because it not only increases yang energy, but also has an effect on yin, blood and Essence. However, the ossified bones that the velvet turns into during autumn have minimal effect.

Ginseng: ginseng is the most famous of all herbs in the world. It is called a "human plant" due to its shape closely resembling the human body and so, according to the Doctrine of Signatures, has a strong effect on the entire human body. As one of the most potent aphrodisiac herbs on the planet, it has strong effects on the *Source Qi*. It is a super tonic for the cardiovascular, respiratory, endocrine and digestive systems.

Other commonly used Qi and yang tonics to increase sexual energy in eastern medicine include:
- Eucommia bark: besides being a strong yang tonic, this bark also treats weakness and pain in the low back and knees.
- Hippocampus (seahorse): another sea animal (yang within yin) that strongly strengthens Kidney yang.

- Epimedium: commonly known as Horny Goat Plant. As the name indicates, this is one of the most famous herbs for boosting sexual energy.
- Cistanche: the stem of this plant, which resembles male genital (Doctrine of Signatures), is used medicinally for impotence, premature ejaculation and frequent urination.
- Cynomorium: this is similar to cistanche in shape and function.
- Psoralea: the fruit and seed of this plant strengthen the Kidneys and digestive system.
- Gecko (toad-headed lizard): strengthens the Kidneys and the respiratory system.
- Cordyceps (Chinese caterpillar fungus): because this herb is part plant and part insect, it has a balance of yin and yang, and so can be used for a long period of time. It is commonly used to invigorate the lung function and strengthen general weakness.
- Chinese leek seed: in general, seeds bring energy to the reproductive system. This seed in particular is black (yin) in color which directly affects the Kidneys.
- Chinese dodder seed: another seed that strongly boosts Kidney Essence.
- Wild Yam: a Qi tonic commonly used for general weakness, nocturnal emission, frequent urination and prolonged diarrhea.

In addition to the qi and yang tonics there is another category of herbs called blood tonics. Most blood tonics do not affect the reproductive system directly but there are a few that do. They include:

- Lycium fruit: this is a raspberry (dried green) commonly known as goji berry. It can raise overall body temperature as mussels do, and especially the temperature of the sexual organs. Lycium also nourishes blood, prevents graying of hair and improves eyesight. It is commonly used for impotence, nocturnal emission, low back and leg pain.
- Morus fruit: also known as mulberry, it tonifies blood and the Kidneys. Commonly used for graying of hair, weakened hearing, dizziness, tinnitus and thirst. It calms the mind as it strengthens sexual energy.
- He Shou Wu (fleeceflower root): this is a famous herb for darkening hair. It is used for the graying of hair due to weakness in bodily functioning,

particularly of the Kidneys. It enhances overall bodily function and nourishes Kidney Essence.

Other herbs commonly used to boost the Jing or Essence include schizandra, euryale seed and rosa fruit. Schizandra fruit resembles the shape of Kidneys (Doctrine of Signatures) and is known to increase libido, support fertility, boost immunity, and enhance liver and respiratory functions. Euryale seed and rosa fruit both have a strong effect on the reproductive system and are commonly used for seminal emission, frequent urination and diarrhea.

Another herb that has been in the news recently as an aphrodisiac is rhodiola rosea, a Siberian plant. Its efficacy has even been featured on The Oprah Winfrey Show by Dr. Mehmet Oz. It is said to boost sexual function by increasing the production of nitric oxide, which was discussed earlier, and by reducing the stress hormone cortisol. Additional benefits according to Dr. Oz include "improving brain function, mood, cardiovascular and immune function, and boosting energy, stamina and endurance."

Remember that in eastern medicine, herbs are not used individually but rather in combinations called herbal formulas or decoctions. Readers are strongly advised to consult with a trained and licensed eastern medicine practitioner for further advice.

To have optimal sexual energy in daily life, we must strive for balance in the mind, body and spirit. Thus, we should:

- ❖ Meditate regularly to get stress and emotions under control, especially those of anger, worry and fear.
- ❖ Maintain a healthy diet and lifestyle.
- ❖ Exercise regularly and take nutritional supplements.
- ❖ Try to avoid cigarettes and excessive intake of alcohol and caffeine.

The Big Picture

Aside from the joy, pleasure, love, intimacy and procreation we derive from sex, proper sex can also be therapeutic and healing. It can help us relax, elevate our spirit, and become a source of bliss, possibly helping us attain enlightenment. Conversely, improper or excessive sexual activity will not only damage our physical health, it will also hinder mental, emotional and spiritual development. The ultimate goal of sex in terms of eastern tradition, therefore, is to unify or unite yin and yang to create a perfect totality called Tai Chi and attune to or resonate with Tao or God.

Western medicine is truly a remarkable science. Its abilities to diagnose, treat and discover are immense. Problems arise, however, when symptoms are seen to be diseases separate from their underlying causes and the overall health of the body is not the primary concern. The eastern medical approach is a holistic guide to follow as it keeps a broad perspective of health.

Although it is sometimes necessary to focus on details, they shouldn't obscure one's vision of the whole. It is only by challenging our limited perspective that we can see the consequences of our actions and live healthier, more productive lives.

CHAPTER 14
Yin and Yang of Obesity

Obesity has become an international crisis of epic proportions and the statistics surrounding this epidemic are mind-boggling. On June 7, 2004, *Time* magazine reported that two-thirds of U.S. adults are overweight and half of them are obese. In addition, one in six children between the ages of 6 and 19 years old is overweight. Not surprisingly, even twenty-five percent of our pets are overweight.

On February 18, 2010, the World Health Organization (WHO) reported that 2.6 million people worldwide die from complications of obesity and excess weight each year equaling 5% of the total number of death worldwide. The WHO also announced that one billion of the 6.8 billion people on Earth are overweight, and in the next five years, this is expected to increase to 1.5 billion.

The problem of obesity is not just one of appearance or aesthetics. Excess weight is dangerous to our health. The National Institute of Health, the Centers for Disease Control and Prevention, and the American Heart Association all issued warnings about the dangers of obesity stating that obesity drastically increases the risk of diseases such as cancer, stroke, heart disease, diabetes, hypertension and osteoarthritis. Furthermore, kidney disease, gall bladder disease, infertility, rheumatism, neuralgia, stomach ulcers, sleep apnea and skin disorders are more commonly found in obese people.

Obesity is the number one cause of increases in our nation's healthcare costs. According to the Surgeon General, "The total medical tab for illnesses related to obesity is $117 billion a year and climbing."[1] Each year, American consumers spend billions of dollars on diet books, consulting diet experts, diet pills, herbal diet teas and meal replacement shakes, exercise equipment and health club memberships, as well as drastic medical procedures such as liposuction and gastric bypass operations, which alone numbered 100,000 in the year 2003.[2]

In response to the problem of obesity, "experts" have developed diets to help us shed pounds. These diets include Atkins, South Beach, Zone, Jenny Craig, Blood-type, Weight Watchers and Slim Fast, just to name a few. Even Dr. Phil has published a weight-loss helper. Yet even with all of these "expert solutions" Americans continue to grow fatter. What is the underlying cause of obesity and why is it getting worse every year? More importantly, what can be done to stop it?

Let us first discuss some of the causes of obesity, applying the holistic eastern perspective of yin and yang.

Causes of Obesity

The causes of obesity come down to simple physics. The more substance we take in (yin) and the less we expend (yang), the more weight we will gain (yin). Thus obesity is due to excess intake and storing of substance and a lack of expenditure of energy.

As with all diseases, the causes of obesity can be looked at in terms of genetic and environmental factors. Genetic factors are considered yin because they are fixed, while environmental factors are considered yang as they are variable. Regardless of the cause, however, an excess of yin relative to yang leads to weight gain and obesity.

1. Genetic Factors

Our genes determine our physical structure, whether we are short and stocky or tall and thin. Some people are predisposed to obesity because of an inherently sluggish metabolism (yin). People with slower metabolisms generally tend to gather and accumulate (yin) energy and mass, making it very easy to put on excess weight and very difficult to burn calories.

Our genes also predispose us to crave salt, sugar and fat and to take in more calories than necessary. From an evolutionary standpoint, when we moved from being hunter-gatherers (yang) to farmer-herders (yin) the transition drastically changed the way we eat and our level of activity.

2. Environmental Factors

Environmental factors can largely be classified into physical, psychological, lifestyle, and socioeconomic factors.

Physical. Technological advancements have caused a severe reduction in physical activity and exercise. People in industrialized countries live in artificial environments. Many of us rarely walk more than 1/10th of a mile per day. This lack of exercise creates a yin condition of the body, creating weight gain and obesity.

Psychological/Behavioral. The chief psychological or behavioral factor influencing obesity involves abnormal eating patterns such as incessant, uncontrolled or compulsive urges and food cravings. These are all yang mental/behavioral traits and are commonly known as "emotional eating" or "binge-eating." In addition, many obese people eat large quantities of food at night. This is the most yin time and thus the most conducive to weight gain. The major cause for these abnormal patterns is mental and/or emotional stress. But there can be underlying physical reasons such as nutritional deficiencies, hormonal imbalances, and non-prescription and prescription drug usage. All of these factors cause imbalances in yin and yang.

Incorrect choice of foods. Mass produced, highly processed and genetically modified foods, excess intake of salt and refined sugar, and excessive fried, greasy foods can all cause obesity. Also, microwaved foods, artificial sweeteners, MSG and other artificial condiments as well as foods that lack fiber can contribute to weight gain.

Incorrect or inconsistent meal schedules. This can also disturb the normal balance, weaken digestive ability and cause obesity.

Socioeconomic factors. Researchers have noted that as more people adopt a western lifestyle, especially the American lifestyle, there is a greater increase in obesity. In general, people of the lower socioeconomic bracket tend to be more obese, mainly due to a lack of time and resources.

Advertisement. TV, radio, billboard and print ads and commercials for food and drinks are ubiquitous, luring us to try products that aren't good for us. According to a *Time* magazine report, by age 17, a child has spent 38% more time in front of the TV than in school, and for every hour of TV a child averages per day, his or her risk for obesity rises by 6%.[3]

Technology. As mentioned above, due to technological advancement, we do not get enough physical exercise.

Superabundance. Compared to the rest of the world, we live in a country that is superabundant in everything, including food.

Easy Access/Convenience. In the U.S. we can get any type of food just about anywhere and at any time of the day for very little money. We can easily get to a local burger stand, a convenience store, or a supermarket 24 hours a day, seven days a week.

Health issues. Hormonal imbalances, diabetes, digestive system weakness, Candida overgrowth, nutritional deficiencies, allergies, parasites, etc. can contribute to obesity.

Drugs. Commonly used drugs such as prednisone and antidepressants are known to cause weight gain.

Consequences of Obesity and Overeating

We need to be aware of the dangers of overeating. Modern research tells us that overeating causes a decrease in the number of T-lymphocytes, our most important immune cell. In addition, our liver cells may become damaged from excessive eating, impairing their ability to detoxify the body and leading to a fatty liver. Brain cells may also become adversely affected by overeating, manifesting in a decrease of overall mental function. Additionally, a major cause of premature aging is overeating. As mentioned earlier, it is also a major cause for diabetes, heart disorders and hypertension. Obesity not only increases the occurrence of diseases but people who are obese also have a higher incidence of accidents and early death.

If these statistics are not cause enough to get us to eat less, here's something else to think about: According to a recent report in *Men's Health* magazine, researchers found that in the past ten years, the sex drive in the U.S. has dropped by thirty-eight percent and obesity is one of the main causes. With weight gain biochemical changes occur that reduce blood flow to the genital region.

Moreover, the ability to procreate or have children is hindered due to damaged sperm and ovulation problems brought about by excessive weight.

Taking into account the health risks, financial concerns and drastic measures many people choose, we can see the severity of the issue facing us.

An Eastern Perspective on Obesity

1. Stress, Comfort Level and Life Cycle

Many people gain weight after they get married. Why? Generally people feel more secure and comfortable after they get married because of mutual love and bonding. Married people are settling down–literally–and this settling down becomes extra weight.

In addition, people are generally thinner when they are younger but by their late thirties to early forties will begin to gain weight. Eastern philosophy explains that this time of life is the beginning of a time of fruition (yin) or harvesting (yin). It is also a time when people become more concerned with financial matters, family issues and material wealth (all yin). People become more materialistic (yin) than they were in their teenage years, a yang period of life, when they were more idealistic. The reason for this is that during our late 30s and early 40s our energy begins to gather inward (yin).

From these examples, we can see that weight gain occurs when there is less stress in our lives or when our metabolisms slow down with age. But what about people who maintain high levels of stress but are still overweight? Why are these people gaining and maintaining weight? And what about people who are thin even in later years? The answer to these questions is that for the thin married couple or mature person stress decreases their appetites, while the opposite is taking place in those who are overweight. Overweight people are probably binging on foods, especially those high in sugar, fats and calories. They are taking comfort in food to either forget about problems or help them relax. Sugar has a particularly relaxing and soothing effect and gives a quick energy boost. It relaxes the body in much the same way as a cigarette to a chain smoker or a drink to an alcoholic.

While stress can impair digestive functioning of both obese and thin people, obese people will retain poorly digested foods as fat while thin people release poorly digested foods quickly through loose stool or diarrhea.

2. Instant Gratification

We live in a fast-paced, get-it-done-yesterday society that thirsts for instant gratification (yang). One outcome of this mentality (or perhaps a contributing factor) is the creation of instant foods, namely candy, chocolate, cookies, ice cream, foods from fast food chains and TV dinners that are saturated with empty calories. The foods we crave the most are very yang in nature, particularly sugar, and give the body instant energy. However, the abundance of these easily accessible, highly-processed foods creates many internal problems.

Eating too many instant foods puts your digestive system in a lazy, sluggish state. Over a period of time, this will weaken it, making it inefficient. An inefficient digestive system is one cause of weight gain. Rugged, raw foods require more effort to digest and therefore help strengthen not only the digestive system but mental functioning as well. Obviously more work means more calories burned. So let's give our digestive systems a workout (yang) and eat more raw foods, while feeding our spirits by eating less overall. The only exception is when a person is ill or needs to gain weight quickly. In this case, a person should eat softer, more easily digestible foods. Otherwise, regular, solid, whole foods are the way to go, just as nature intended.

3. Too Much Gluttony

People eat food for many reasons. We eat when we are hungry (a form of desire) but we also eat to satisfy other desires, relieve tension or boredom, circumvent buried emotions, etc. Food is easily accessible, relatively inexpensive and provides instant gratification. We crave the energy and pleasure we obtain from eating and we tend to overdo it. In fact, humans tend to overdo anything that provides pleasure.

What we need is a new revelation about food. We need to reacquaint ourselves with food and relearn its value in the scope of our lives. We also need to understand why we eat and what the consequences are when we do not eat properly. We should honestly ask ourselves just what food is.

4. Slackening of the Mind

As with any health issue, the number one cause of obesity is a slackening of the mind, body and spirit leading to a lack of awareness of what we are doing to our bodies. This is simply ignorance, laziness, fatigue, and apathy. Let's look at the typical "couch potato." This man spends his day or weekend watching football and eating potato chips, cookies, pizza and soda in addition to three regular meals. Most likely this man is obese. Being ignorant, this man has lost contact with his higher self and is either not aware or is in denial of the harm he is inflicting on himself.

We live in a nation with plenty of resources and goods, available to us 24/7. We have forgotten or are ignorant of what scarcity means. One outcome of abundance and easy accessibility is the slackening of the mind. Like a "spoiled child" whose needs have been met unconditionally, we have lost control over ourselves with an overabundance of food.

5. Imbalance in the Source Energy

Eastern medicine discusses a fundamental, essential form of energy called *Source Qi* (Refer to Chapters 3 and 13). This energy is responsible for maintaining the homeostasis of the body. It is also the healing mechanism of the body. The quality as well as the quantity (longevity) of our lives is determined by this energy. When Source energy is weakened because of improper lifestyle or stress it cannot control our appetite. Our instincts go haywire and cannot decipher what foods to eat or when or how much to eat. Modern science refers to this condition as an imbalance in the hypothalamus, the body's internal thermostat for body weight. Some people's baseline is set higher while others are set lower. Those who have a higher set point will gain weight more easily and vice versa. And just as the amount of Source energy can fluctuate, the set point of our internal thermostat can change throughout our lifetime.

Yin and Yang Way to Lose Weight

As with all aspects of health maintenance, the key to losing weight and keeping it off is to balance our internal yin and yang with a two-prong approach. First, we should nurture the yin aspect of our minds–thinking more about long term (yin) health benefits and less about instant gratification. We need to take things more slowly (yin), one step at a time. And we should reduce our desires (yang), especially for material things.

Second, we have to nurture the yang aspect of our bodies by moving, exercising and working more–walking instead of driving, taking the stairs instead of the elevator, and doing some form of physical work like gardening, cleaning, carrying grocery bags, etc.

Proper Eating: Spiritual Aspect

A one-size-fits-all approach to weight loss is ineffective; we need individualized programs. But as with all things in life, the best solution is balance and harmony by practicing moderation. An overall healthy lifestyle and behavior changes are needed. The most important changes to make are in our minds and spirits.

1. Taking One Step at a Time

There are few quick fixes (yang) in life. Most things take time. We should take everything one step at a time (yin). It is important to set a realistic goal and move positively and consistently towards it in small increments. We should remember the saying, "Easy come; easy go." This applies to weight loss as well. The faster we lose weight, the faster and more likely it is that it will return. But if we work at it one step at a time (yin), allowing our bodies to adjust slowly to the weight loss, the weight loss will be more permanent (yin). If we take drastic measures with certain fad diets, diet pills or surgery, we can seriously damage our organs and health.

2. Reducing Our Gluttony

We must reduce our gluttony, or excessive greed (yin) for food. Exercising frugality, especially with food, is very important. The Bible says, "A man does not live by bread alone." The more food we eat, the more animal-like we become; the less we eat, the more spiritual we become. We stand at a crossroad every time we eat. To put it bluntly, we ought to ask ourselves each and every time we eat, "Am I going to be a more spiritual person (yang) or more animal-like (yin)?" The answer will be obvious. We ought to make the right choice each time. So every meal or snack time is a time to exercise our spirit, discipline and willpower. We should eat just enough to get by. That is all it takes. No more, no less!

We have to eat to live and not live to eat. Let food be the fuel and nourishment for our bodies, minds and spirits. We can find joy and delight in food, but let us not overindulge in it. We must find solace, comfort, satisfaction and satiety not from a physical source like food but from a spiritual source. We should find joy and delight in the spirit. We should reward ourselves with things other than food. There are other energy sources like exercise or meditating that actually might "taste" better than food. We should remember that, as long as we take in adequate nutrients and appropriate calories for our activity level, the less food we eat, the more we deposit in the savings account of our soul.

Every time we exercise the right choice, our bodies, minds and spirits will become more empowered and enlightened. Let us not become a slave to food– we have to be the master of our food just as we have to be master of our destiny. All in all, the less food we eat, the healthier we will be. This is a dietary principle that is absolutely free of any side effects with no cost to us.

The bottom line is this: If our spirit does not wake up and take charge, no diet or exercise will work. We should try to practice moderation, which means a yin-yang balanced approach, and eat moderately, wisely and conscientiously.

3. Develop More Reverence for Food

We need to have more respect for our bodies and develop more reverence for our foods. We should not take food for granted. Something–either animal or plant–sacrificed its life so that we could live on. It is quite shocking and saddening to hear that over five million children worldwide die from hunger every year. Approximately one child every seven seconds or 14,000 children die of hunger and malnourishment every day and more than 70% of world's population has trouble getting one meal a day due to famine and extreme poverty. We should think about this and have more gratitude for the food on our table.

4. Give Gratitude

We should be thankful and express love for what we have. This applies not only to diet but to all aspects of our daily life. We should not take anything for granted. Saying a prayer or meditating before we eat not only tunes us in to the correct frame of mind in which to properly digest and assimilate our foods, but it also communicates our appreciation to nature or God and to those that have made the ultimate sacrifice (animal or plant) for our life. We should also try to give thanks or say prayers after meals. In this way we develop sacred reverence and express gratitude for what we have ingested. We believe this should be the number one rule in our diet, regardless of which one we choose to follow.

5. Eat Only After Some Form of Work: Physical, Mental or Spiritual

Back in the former Soviet Union days, an important motto was: "If you don't work, you don't eat." This is actually really good advice, especially for those trying to lose weight.

There was an interesting experiment involving two groups of rats. One group ate whenever food was available. After a short time, all the rats in this group became fat, lazy, sluggish and dull. The other group was fed only after a certain test and problem solving task. In stark contrast to the first group, the rats in this group were healthy, alert and active.

We should try to earn our meals. In this way, we will develop more appreciation for the food on our table. Ultimately, eating becomes more special and we will experience true joy and bliss from it.

All in all, spiritual cultivation takes time. We should do it slowly, one step at a time and one day at a time. A thousand mile journey begins with a single step. We should start with simple things and move on to more complex matters. And we should always remember the famous adage, "Eat to live; don't live to eat."

6. Fasting

All religions practice one form or another of fasting. This is practiced to develop and cultivate more reverence and devotion to God. There is more time for spiritual practice and less time and energy spent digesting food.

It is a fact that fasting benefits health and longevity. Another rodent experiment proved this point. This experiment demonstrated the benefits of a low calorie diet with two groups of rats. One group was fed high-calorie, highly nutritious foods, loaded with protein, vitamins, minerals, etc. Another group was fed a low-calorie diet. After several weeks rats from both groups were placed in a pool of water and made to swim until they drowned. Not surprisingly, the low-calorie group out-swam the high calorie group. Other rats from the low-calorie groups that had not drowned outlived the high calorie group.

Fasting has both physical (yin) and mental (yang) benefits. Physically, our bodies will have an increased ability to withstand disease because our cells will work harder to live with a limited supply of nutrients. With fewer nutrients our cells' survival instincts become stronger and more capable of warding off foreign invaders. For the same reason, the body will also quickly discard diseased and old cells.

Psychologically, when we eat less our minds become clearer, our focus more acute and our memory, comprehension and awareness improve. In addition, our pride and ego are held in check. We become more humble because we experience the feebleness of our bodies as our overall energy initially declines. Anger and frustration decline as well and we become less anxious as every cell in the body wakes up and is more alert to see a bigger picture of life.

During fasting we experience a calming of the mind; excess mental and emotional clutter fades. The ability to understand our purpose in life increases and we become empowered, inspired and enlightened. We never hear of a sage or saint becoming enlightened during a feast. Our spiritual soul (yang) becomes activated and thrives while the lower animal soul (yin) weakens. The end result is the purification of our soul.

We do not have to be on a total fast; it can be partial, perhaps one or two very small meals per day for several days. Complete juice fasting is also very good for a few days. We do not have to starve ourselves for 40 days and 40 nights. But if we decide to go on a total fast, we should always seek the advice of healthcare practitioners who are well versed in fasting. Every little thing counts, so the more we make an effort at reducing food intake, the more alive and healthier we will become.

Let's face it. No matter how much experts tell us how our diet is devitalized, there are just too many calories and too many nutrients (carbohydrates, fats and proteins) in the typical American diet. In certain parts of the world, people live and work with just one bowl of rice and water daily (this is not a healthy diet either but it is in stark contrast to the American diet.) We have to continue to be vigilant of how much we eat and stop ingesting excessive nutrients since all surplus nutrients are stored as fat or toxin.

All spiritual traditions teach us the principle of "Redemption of the soul from the body," and one of the most important facets to this principle is fasting.

Healthy Eating Habits

1. We should use mealtimes to cultivate and feed our minds and spirits, and not just our bellies. By staying *present* and *mindful* of our foods at mealtimes, we are making each mealtime a time to exercise and renew our spirits. We should not watch TV, read the paper, drive, or let our minds wander away from the food we are eating. We should remain fully aware, thoroughly tasting each and every bite until we complete our meals. Also, we should take care to appreciate the appearance and aroma of our foods. This mindfulness also applies to the preparation of our foods, which should be done with the utmost care and respect. If we are serving food, we should do this with a calm and serene frame of mind, with complete focus.

2. We should eat slower and always chew our foods well. By chewing well, we improve our digestion and assimilation while at the same time conserving bodily energy and achieving a feeling of fullness sooner. We are also exercising our patience by eating slowly and chewing each bite carefully. We should remember that undigested food turns into fat. We should try to make a habit of chewing 30 times per mouthful. Though this may sound like a lot, it will benefit us in many ways. For those of us with digestive problems, eastern medicine recommends chewing up to 100 times. This will strengthen our system. Also, we should remember not to talk when we are chewing. In fact, we should try to reduce talking during meals—staying fully focused on the food, then talking afterwards.

3. We should try to relax when we eat. We ought to make sure that we are sitting at the table with good posture (not slouched over). We should not eat standing up, lying down, in the car or in front of the TV or computer.

4. It is best not to eat when we are upset or emotionally distraught. If we eat when disturbed, we will lose appreciation for our foods. Furthermore, by diverting attention away from our foods, we will also divert energy and blood away from our digestive system, leading to decreased efficiency in assimilation and absorption of nutrients. We should either skip the meal altogether or wait a few hours until we can calm down and settle into the right frame of mind. By extension, it is best to eat in the most peaceful surroundings we can create, either alone or in the company of people with whom we resonate. To help us relax, we can play soothing, relaxing classical music during meals. We should

make sure to keep our emotions calm at all times, but especially during mealtimes.

5. We should not eat when we are not hungry. When we are not hungry, our digestive system is not ready to accept any food, and instead, needs to rest. This is especially true when we become sick, such as from a common cold. As a natural response to illness, our bodies conserve the energy it would normally use to digest food so that it can fight the invading pathogen.

6. We should never eat right before going to bed. As previously stated, we should never eat right before going to bed. The daytime is the active or yang time, so it is the time when we should let the digestive organs do their work. During the night (yin) everything slows down, so we should likewise give the digestive system a rest. Remember that our liver performs its detoxifying action when we sleep at night. If we eat before bedtime, then the liver has to spend its energy digesting foods rather than detoxifying impurities.

Food that is not digested during the night will sit and ferment in our intestines. This will create a foul gas that will cause burping as well as abdominal distention and fullness. In eastern medicine this is called food stagnation. Food stagnation can cause several problems ranging from obesity to personality disorders. Since the energy in the digestive system cannot move freely, our mental and emotional energies become blocked, causing further stagnation. It is best, therefore, to eat our last meal at least three to four hours before sleeping.

7. We should never fill our stomach to full capacity. We should be very conscious about this. It is best to always leave the table feeling a little hungry. We should fill only seventy-five percent of the stomach's capacity. Eating less translates into better health, not just physically but also mentally. Our true spirit will function more actively and with greater clarity if we eat less. This is because any energy not needed for the digestive process will "roll over" into the savings account of our soul. Thus, many people in various religions and philosophies practice fasting to cultivate, elevate and purify their bodies, minds, souls and spirits.

Another reason why we should not fill our stomach to its maximum capacity is that we should leave room for the energy of the digestive system to move freely. When we fill our stomach completely, there is little room for the energy to move properly. This leads to stagnation and incomplete digestion, both of which can easily lead to disease, including obesity. Belching, hiccupping, difficulty in swallowing, nausea, vomiting and heartburn (cases in which the energy is not properly descending), or flatulence, diarrhea, and distention are some early symptoms. If left unchecked, the body may develop more serious conditions, including prolapsed organs, ulcers or gastritis.

We should also be aware of other signs of improper or poor digestion including pain or discomfort in the abdomen, bad breath or foul taste in the mouth, excess phlegm, runny nose or nasal congestion, headaches, heaviness of the head, skin blemishes and rashes, and problems in urination or bowel movement.

8. We should begin physical or mental activity slowly after our meals. It is best to either rest quietly or take an easy stroll for a few minutes (up to 15 minutes). This will aid our digestion.

9. It is important to eat breakfast. The morning is a yang or active time when the body is burning fuel most efficiently and thus it is the proper time to provide fuel to the body. In fact, researchers are finding out that our bodies best utilize the nutrients such as protein and carbohydrates in the morning. By eating breakfast, we will improve our overall mental functioning such as decision making, memory and concentration, as well as elevate our moods. By contrast, the evening is a yin time and is the time of slowing down and storing. Thus, as mentioned above, eating late at night is counterproductive to good health.

If we skip breakfast, we are breaking a natural rhythm and will end up eating more in the latter part of day (yin), which will be burned at a slower (yin) rate. Here, our bodies are overcompensating for the deficit created in the morning. In some traditions, food is only consumed during the yang part of the day (midnight to before noon), a time when the food can be properly burned and utilized.

Thus, it is wise to follow the saying, "Eat breakfast like a king, lunch like a prince and dinner like a pauper." Making our second meal the largest meal is also a sound dietary practice. It is most important to maintain the smallest meal during dinner. There is a similar old Russian maxim that goes, "Breakfast, eat by yourself; lunch, share it with a friend; and dinner, give it to your enemy." To help us lose weight, we should eat only between sunrise and sunset (ideally before 6 p.m.).

10. We should learn to read, properly identify and interpret ingredients on food labels. In addition to the overall calories and salt content in the ingredients, we should avoid any food with trans fats such as hydrogenated or partially-hydrogenated oils, corn syrup, high fructose corn syrup, MSG, and other chemical food additives and preservatives such as sodium nitrates.

11. We should carefully plan out our meal schedule and food. We should not skip meals. Doing things haphazardly will bring about haphazard results. It is best to keep a diary of our food intake and our physical and emotional feelings. Keeping a journal to track and evaluate our eating habits is very important to making steady and lasting progress. It is also good to weigh ourselves daily.

12. As we get older our metabolism and physical activities slow down, we burn calories less efficiently and retain more weight. This is an important reason why we should reduce our intake of food as we age. Our bodies require fewer calories to function optimally with age.

Choosing Healthy Foods

1. We should remember to keep a "Middle Path" approach to our dietary regimen. This means moderating the amount of food we eat, as well as moderating the variety of foods we eat. We should neither restrict ourselves to a single food group nor mix too many food groups at one sitting.

2. We should have some form of protein for breakfast. According to researchers at St. Louis University, eating a breakfast consisting of two eggs and two slices of bread caused subjects to eat fewer calories during the day.

3. We should eat whole foods whenever possible. There are two meanings to this. First, we should consume a wide variety of foods: grains, legumes, seeds, nuts, fruits, vegetables, etc., as this type of diet is the most effective means to derive balanced nutrients. Second, we should eat foods in their original state, with everything or as much intact as possible. For example, when eating small fish, such as sardines or anchovies, eat the whole fish, complete with head, bones and skin. Organically grown fruits without pesticides and whole grains with the germ layer intact, such as whole brown rice, whole wheat,

etc., are also essential to a healthy diet. According to a study performed at Pennsylvania State University, eating more whole grains such as oatmeal, whole brown rice and barley will help us lose belly fat and reduce the risk of certain chronic diseases such as heart attacks and strokes.

4. We should try to grow, buy and eat one hundred percent organic foods. We should reduce as much as we can our consumption of genetically modified foods, homogenized and pasteurized products, as well as microwaved foods, farm-raised fish, etc. We should try to reduce eating out at restaurants, and instead eat more homemade foods.

5. It is best to eat solid foods. Our bodies were designed to digest them, and we will only grow healthier by consuming them. On the other hand, if we overeat processed, softened foods, our overall health will suffer.

6. We should try to eat all five flavors during each meal. Eastern medicine discusses five flavors, which include sour, pungent, sweet, bitter and salty, plus an additional one called puckering or astringent flavor. Our bodies will be better balanced if all of these flavors are included in our meals.

7. We should drink green tea. Its health benefits have been well documented. In the East, people drink green tea on a regular basis because it is said to "melt the fat or the grease." Green tea can increase mental acuity, stimulate our metabolism, regulate our hunger and detoxify our bodies.

8. Our bodies are approximately seventy percent water. Correspondingly, we should include foods that have high moisture content, similar in composition to our bodies. Consumption of fruits and vegetables are extremely important in this regard.

Having said this, it is important to qualify a couple of points. It is best to eat fruits not as a part of our regular meals, but at least one hour before or several hours after meals because of the different digestive enzymes required to process them. If you have to eat fruits with your meals, try to eat as little as possible and reserve them for the end of the meal.

9. We should drink 8 to 10 glasses of water daily between meals. Properly hydrating our system will help facilitate waste elimination by the kidneys and more efficiently metabolize fat. We should not drink large amounts of water

with our meals. We should limit ourselves to one cup of water, slowly sipped, during the meal. Water will dilute our digestive juices, raising the pH of our stomach, and making digestion less efficient.

10. We should consider the formation of our teeth. People have on average 16 molars, eight incisors and four canines. Molars are for grinding down grains and legumes, incisors are for biting and cutting vegetables and fruits, and canines are for cutting meat. We should set up our diet according to the ratio established by our teeth: 4 to 2 to 1. Our diet should consist of approximately fifty percent grains, five percent legumes/seeds/nuts, ten percent fruits, twenty percent vegetables and fifteen percent meat/fish/poultry. We should remember that these are not fixed numbers; if you are a vegetarian or vegan, for example, you can eliminate the last category of foods, and raise the percentage of other foods proportionately.

Maintaining a Healthy Lifestyle

1. Exercise. We need to perform physical (yang) exercises every day to keep our bodies healthy. We also need to exercise our minds/souls/spirits (yin) every day. There should always be a yin-yang balance in physical exercises. Thus we should perform yang-type exercises such as weight training and calisthenics for strength building and aerobics for endurance, as well as yin-type exercises such as Tai Chi, Yoga, Qigong and walking for relaxation and calming of the mind. We can think of both types of exercises in terms of the speed at which they are performed: fast-paced workouts are yang while slow-paced exercises are yin. For balance, try to practice both forms of exercises on a daily basis.

The benefits of exercise are too numerous to list entirely. Walking, for instance, will lower our blood pressure and blood sugar. We should try to walk for at least 40 to 50 minutes per day, five to six days per week. As we walk, our breathing should deepen and the body should sweat a little. However we should be able to carry on a comfortable conversation while walking. Additionally, we can help ourselves more if we try to walk to lunch, avoid elevators and get off one stop earlier on buses. Performing weight lifting exercises to build muscles can help a great deal in weight loss as muscles burn more calories. Stretching exercises not only improve overall circulation but also will eliminate bodily tension and help open our minds.

2. Get Proper Amount of Sleep. Studies have shown that those who sleep less than six and a half hours per night were more likely to be obese than those who slept longer. This is due to the fluctuations in two hormones known as leptin which suppresses appetite and ghrelin which stimulates appetite.

3. Practice Deep Breathing Daily. Studies have shown that oxygenating our system can actually help us lose weight. There is an increased metabolism and efficient functioning of all systems of the body with greater uptake of oxygen.

4. Meditate Regularly. One of the best ways to calm the yang or active mind is to meditate. Meditation will open up our minds, giving us a broader perspective on life, health and food. It is all about balance. Obesity is no different. If we balance our yin and yang, we will lose weight. Meditation is conducive to just that.

5. Reduce TV Viewing Time. Take a break from the news and non-educational shows on TV. Utilize the time for exercise and other beneficial activities like meditation and studying. Studies have shown that watching more than 2 hours of TV per day increases the tendency for adults to take in more calories (by roughly 7%) and to eat more sweets.

Conclusion

The theory of yin and yang can be applied to every aspect of daily life from diet to politics, as well as, every phenomena and form in the universe. Although challenging, the application of this theory brings about a more complete understanding of life and our place in this world. Learning to step back and contemplate this ancient theory gives us a tool with which we can deepen our knowledge of the inner workings of the universe and gain perspective on our personal, social and professional relationships.

The importance of perspective cannot be understated. It is as important as an open heart and an open mind when attempting to see the totality or Tai Chi of any situation. In maintaining an open heart and mind we can actually transcend the duality of yin and yang. Ultimately, with a deeper understanding and the daily practice of yin-yang theory, you will be led to the great path known as Tao, the goal of all eastern philosophies and religions. Being able to see and realize the interconnectedness of everything, the great web of the universe, and the unity of all things is what life is all about. We have to relent and surrender our basic biases and return to our true nature, which is Tao.

Use the yin-yang principle as a tool, a guide in life's journey. Allow its principles to help you navigate through and understand life's trials and tribulations as well as its joys and pleasures. Learn to accept these life's ups and downs with the realization that life is nothing other than interplay between yin and yang. See, feel and embrace the yin within yang and yang within yin.

In closing, we would like to share a very famous story about life's ups and downs from the East, called "The old man and his horse."

> There was an old man living on the border of a country. This man had a beautiful horse. He loved his horse so much

that he groomed it every day and took very good care of it. One day, without warning, his horse ran away. The old man was devastated. When the townspeople heard they all said, "Bad omen." A few days later, the horse returned with a companion, another fine horse. The old man was elated. When the townspeople heard they all said, "Good luck." This old man had a teenage son who wanted to break in the new horse. While riding the horse, the man's son was thrown and broke his leg. When the townspeople heard they all said, "Bad luck." Soon after the young man's fall the country was thrust into war with a neighboring country. The army recruited all of the young men for service. However, when the recruiters came to the old man's house, they left after seeing that the old man's son was injured and would not be able to fight. When the battle broke out all of the young men who had been recruited from the town were killed. The old man counted his blessings.

Notes

Chapter 2

    1. Eastern physiognomy discovers a person's nature and destiny by analyzing the shape of eyes, ears, nose and mouth as well as the whole face according to the principle of the *I Ching*. It is similar to western palm reading (palmistry).

Chapter 3

    1. Garvy, John W. *Yin and Yang: Two Hands Clapping*. Newtonville: Wellbeing Books, Vol. 2, 1985, p. 8

    2. Ibid

Chapter 4

    1. Taylor, Jill Bolte. *My Stroke of Insight*. New York: Plume Books, 2009

Chapter 9

    1. Campbell, Don. *The Mozart Effect*. New York: Avon Books, 1997, pp. 82-83

    2. Ibid, p. 14

Chapter 12

    1. *The Merck Manual*, 17th Edition, Whitehouse Station: Merck Research Laboratories, 1999, p. 1410

    2. Channel 9 KCAL News in L.A., June 7th, 2003

    3. Wang, So-jin, *Dongeui Nandal Journal*, Vol. 21, 2005, p. 21

    4. Ibid

Chapter 13

    1. *The Merck Manual*, 17th Edition, Whitehouse Station: Merck Research Laboratories, 1999, p. 2009

Chapter 14
 1. *Time*, June 27, 2004, p. 60
 2. Ibid, p. 60
 3. Ibid, pp. 63, 89

Select Bibliography

Korean

Chun, Chang Sun and Uh, Yoon Hyung, *What is Yin and Yang?* Seoul: Seki publishing, 1994.

Ibid, *What are Five Elements?* Seoul: Seki publishing, 1994.

Han, Kyu Sung, *Discourse on the Principles of I Ching.* Seoul: Eastern Culture Publishing, 1989.

Kim, Hong Kyung, *Self Healing.* Seoul: Shikmoolchoojang Publication, 2000.

Shin, Jae Yong, *Strengthening Sexual Energies in Men.* Seoul: Doong Ji Publication, 1994.

English

Bentov, Itzhak, *Stalking the Wild Pendulum.* Rochester: Destiny Books, 1988.

Chinese Acupuncture and Moxibustion. Beijing: Foreign Languages Press, 1987.

Cho, Hun Young. *Oriental Medicine: A Modern Interpretation.* Translated and revised by, Joseph Kihyon Kim. Compton, Calif.: Yuin University Press, 1996.

Fung, Yu-Lan. *A Short History of Chinese Philosophy.* New York: Free Press, 1966.

Garvy, Jr., John W, *Yin and Yang: Two Hand Clapping.* Newtonville: Wellbeing Books, 1985.

Jilin Liu, *Chinese Dietary Therapy*. New York: Churchill Livingstone, 1995.

Kim, Joseph K. *Compass of Health*. Los Angeles: Heal and Soul, 2010.

Lu, Henry C. *Chinese System of Food Cures*. New York: Sterling Publishing, 1986.

Palmer, Martin, *Yin & Yang: Understanding the Chinese Philosophy of Opposites and How to Apply It to Your Everyday Life*. London: Judy Piaktus (Publishers) Ltd., 1997.

Pitchfold, Paul, *Healing With Whole Foods*. Berkeley: North Atlantic Books, 1993.

Tierrra, Michael, *The Way of Herbs*. New York: Pocket Books, 1998.

Wilhelm, Richard. *I Ching*. Princeton: Princeton University Press, 1990.

Acknowledgments

The authors wish to express our sincere gratitude to the following people whose contributions of time, energy, guidance and support have made this book possible.

Dr. Joseph K. Kim:

I would like to thank Naomi Gelperin Richman, a licensed acupuncturist practicing in Scottsdale, Arizona, for her clear insight and meticulous editing of the entire manuscript. She has previously edited two of my earlier books. I could not have finished the book without her invaluable and wholehearted help.

Robin Schiesser, a licensed acupuncturist practicing in Boulder, Colorado, for her keen observations, meticulous proof reading and thorough editing of the entire manuscript.

Seth Gold, Kim Moraes, Jonathan Gelperin and my niece, Christine Chung, for reading, commenting on and editing the earlier version of this book.

My teacher, Professor Jae Yong Shin, for his inspiration, wisdom, and encouragement.

Mr. Soo Ahn Kim, a freelance artist, for his help with many of the drawings that accompany the text.

Mr. Sammy Silberstein, a graphic designer, for the cover design and layout of the entire book, as well as many of the diagrams and drawings in the book.

Finally, I would like to thank my wife, Anne, for her love and unremitting support on this project.

Dr. David S. Lee:

I would also like to thank all of the people mentioned above who have edited, commented on and read the manuscript.

My teachers, Master Jae Hyung Lee and Master Tae Hoon Kwon, for their profound and wise teachings in Tao, medicine and martial arts.

Finally, I would like to thank my dear wife, Julia, for her unwavering love and support.

About the Authors

Joseph K. Kim, L. Ac., OMD, Ph.D.

As a third generation practitioner of Eastern medicine, Dr. Joseph K. Kim has been enthralled by the *I Ching* and Eastern philosophy for more than 30 years. He served as a Chairman for the Department of Oriental Medicine at Emperor's College of Traditional Oriental Medicine in Santa Monica, California, and is a former acupuncture researcher at the University of California at Irvine, where he studied the effects of acupuncture on brain activity as revealed by a functional MRI.

Dr. Kim has written and translated four books: *Oriental Medicine: A Modern Interpretation*, *An Introduction to Sasang Constitutional Medicine*, *Compass of Health: Using the Art of Sasang Medicine to Maximize Your Health*, and *Science and Tao of I Ching* (co-authored with Dr. David S. Lee).

Dr. Kim also possesses more than 30 years of martial arts training, including Qi Gong and Tai Chi. He served as team doctor for the 1988 United States Tae Kwon Do team (ITF). He maintains a private practice in Encino, California.

David S. Lee, MD, OMD, Ph.D.

Since his teenage years, Dr. David S. Lee has been deeply intrigued by Eastern philosophy, religion and mysticism. Since then he studied the disciplines of Tao, meditation and the martial arts from many teachers. He is one of the chief disciples of both Master Jae Hyung Lee and Master Tae Hoon Kwon, two of the most celebrated and revered Taoist masters of Korea.

Dr. Lee began his study of Eastern medicine from a profound desire to apply his insights and experiences for the betterment of mankind. After receiving advanced degrees in Korea, he moved to US and taught at several acupuncture colleges in the subjects of acupuncture, herbal medicine, Qi Gong and Tai Chi. Feeling a need to link the perspective of traditional Eastern medicine to those of modern medicine, Dr. Lee earned his MD degree.

Dr. Lee has served as a professor at the prestigious Kyung Hee University in Seoul, Korea, and conducted research at both the University of California at Irvine and the Kwang Ju Institute of Science and Technology in Korea. Currently, Dr. Lee maintains a private practice in Seoul, Korea.

For more information on Dr. Kim's or Dr. Lee's seminars and books, please inquire at:

www.yinyangoflife.com
iching38@att.net